FIFTY WAYS TO
LEAVE YOUR LIVER

FIFTY WAYS TO LEAVE YOUR LIVER

The Confessions of an Unjustified Drinker

Tom Shields

BLACK & WHITE PUBLISHING

First published 2009
by Black & White Publishing Ltd
29 Ocean Drive, Edinburgh EH6 6JL

1 3 5 7 9 10 8 6 4 2   09 10 11 12 13

ISBN: 978 1 84502 275 4

A CIP catalogue record for this book is available from the British Library.

Typeset by Ellipsis Books Ltd, Glasgow
Printed and bound by MPG Books Ltd, Bodmin

Contents

Contents

1

'Is life worth living? It all depends on the liver.' — William James

'Why don't you write your autobiography?' asked a friend, who obviously thinks I have lived an interesting life.

So I looked back across my life, and in my typical, self-deprecatory, Scottish, Roman, Calvinist guilt-ridden style, I concluded that my life could be edited down to this short narrative: I got drunk, I got fat, I got sick.

Getting drunk and getting fat was not my full-time occupation ... though I did spend a lot of time and money on these pursuits.

I work as a journalist. Not the kind of journalist who rights wrongs. The closest I got to making a difference was in 1978 during a strike by Glasgow bus drivers.

I happened to take a phone call one day in the newsroom. It

was from one of the striking bus drivers, saying I should take a look at what was going on at a factory where blind people were employed to make furniture.

Strathclyde Bus Company, which in those pre-Thatcher days was still in public ownership, ran a daily service getting the workers to and from the factory. The drivers offered to keep this special

> **3. A Perfect Cure for Drunkenness.**—Let those who are accustomed to the excessive use of ardent spirits, and who wish to stop the practice, I say, let such have a cup of this tea made, as above directed, and drink a part of it immediately on rising in the morning, and the balance just before meal time, keeping entirely away from the places of temptation, they will find a warm, healthy glow spreading from the stomach over the whole system, with a desire for food instead of "rot-gut." Follow this up faithfully, two or three times daily, or whenever the *craving* begins for the accustomed stimulus, for a few days or *weeks*, if necessary, and it will be found that the cayenne, which is the purest stimulant in the whole Materia Medica, with its assistant, the bayberry, which stimulate without an after *prostration*, have gradually *supplied and satisfied* the previous false appetite or cravings of the stomach; whilst the combination has *toned* up the stomach, together with the whole system, AND AGAIN YOU FIND YOURSELF A MAN. But remember, oh, remember! *your only safety is in keeping entirely away from places where intoxicating spirits are kept or sold!*
>
> A *burned* child will not play with fire. I would to God that a burned *man* was equally wise. For not *one* in a *thousand* can resist the solicitation of enemies, (called friends,) to take a glass, just *one*, and that one glass acts like *fresh coals* upon *extinguished* bands, and the fire goes ahead again with a hundred-fold more energy than if thrown upon wood which had never been charred; hence, the propriety of the sentence, "plucked as a brand from the everlasting burnings,"—for if *re-kindled*, there is but little prospect of another extinguishment of the raging fire. Dr. Thompson, notwithstanding all that has been said against him, has done more good than any other medical man that ever lived; for he set the people to studying for themselves.

service running throughout the dispute. The bus company refused.

When I asked why, a spokesperson said: 'We cannot make an exception for these people, even though they are blind.' This was in the days before company spokespeople were sent on expensive media training courses and taught how to avoid making such crass pronouncements.

With no buses available, the workers were being transported in the factory's furniture vans. It was not a difficult story to cover. We had poignant photographs of people, clutching their white sticks, being led up the ramp into the back of a lorry.

They stood, holding on to ropes for balance and looking out with eyes that could not see, as the doors were closed on them for a dangerous and uncomfortable journey. These images of people being loaded like cattle and the incredible comment that a public utility could not make a special case for blind people had an immediate impact. The bus service was resumed the day the story appeared on the front page of the *Glasgow Herald*.

This story should have given me an appetite for campaigning journalism and a burning desire to protect the downtrodden and oppressed. But another opportunity had presented itself. The *Glasgow Herald* had always had, in its 200 years or so of existence, a Diary column which allowed the writer to pursue issues from a not entirely serious viewpoint.

The business of seeking out humorous stories and anecdotes was arduous. It involved many lunches and dinners and spending much time drinking with 'contacts'. The definition of contact, for the purposes of a journalist's expenses claim, is someone who happened to be in a pub at the same time as you.

The allowances were generous, if not quite on the scale of those which British politicians bestow upon themselves. There is not much in the way of moral high ground, scarcely a hillock, from which journalists can berate members of parliament for abuse of expense allowances.

The most we can say is that while MPs have been busy stealing public money, journalists have been picking the pockets of capitalist newspaper barons. This is usually done in agreement with the newspaper barons who, in years gone by but less so today, were happy to throw their wage slaves some scraps from the table.

My happiest days, in terms of the weekly packet stuffed with banknotes, or 'drink vouchers' as we called them, was when Tiny Rowland's Lonrho owned the *Herald*. Tiny was described by Ted Heath as the 'unacceptable face of capitalism.' But he was just generous Uncle Tiny to us.

Ted Heath may have been unhappy because he wasn't getting a brown envelope each week from Tiny Rowland.

The present owners of the *Herald* newspapers are much more careful with their money. Should any of my previous employers consider suing me for any sums of money I claimed that were not spent entirely in pursuit of company business, I warn that they will be hit by a contrary law suit.

I will be seeking punitive damages because they failed in their duty of care towards me. They must have been aware, from reading the details of the food and drink on my expense forms, that I was ruining my health.

My employers should have known I was getting drunk and getting fat entirely on their behalf.

I should point out that not once in all those years was I ever forced at gunpoint to enter a restaurant. At no time did my family have to pay a ransom to have me released from captivity in a pub. It was great fun apart from the occasional depression.

Oscar Wilde said: 'Moderation is a fatal thing. Nothing succeeds like excess.' But poor Oscar died when he was forty-six.

The decline in my health, mostly due to the over-consumption of food and alcohol, was gradual enough for me to ignore. Gout was painful but not life-threatening.

Sleep apnea, the chronic snoring condition, means neither you nor anyone in the vicinity get a decent night's rest. But it is only fatal if your partner stabs you to death or you fall asleep at the wheel of your car.

When I was diagnosed with type 2 diabetes, I coped by *not* reading the details of the nasty side effects.

Then came the alarm bell I could not ignore. My GP, alerted by the onset of diabetes, ordered a full set of blood tests.

'We are a bit concerned about your liver function,' he said when the results came back. The news was not unexpected.

I had seen it so often from the sidelines as colleagues, some of

> **If apparently Dead from Intense Cold.**—Rub the body with ice snow, or cold water. Restore warmth by slow degrees; and, after some time, if necessary, employ the means recommended for the apparently drowned. It is *highly dangerous* to apply heat too early.
> **If apparently Dead from Hanging.**—In addition to the means recommended for the apparently drowned, *bleeding* should early be employed by a medical assistant.
> **If apparently Dead from Noxious Vapors, Lightning, etc.**—Remove the body into a cold fresh air. Dash cold water on the neck, face, and breast frequently. If the body be cold, apply warmth, as recommended for the apparently drowned. Use the means for inflating the lungs as directed above. Let electricity (particularly in accidents from lightning) be early employed by a medical assistant.
> **If apparently Dead from Intoxication.**—Lay the body on a bed, with the head raised; remove the neckcloth and loosen the clothes. Obtain instantly medical assistance, in the meantime apply cloths soaked in cold water to the head, and bottles of hot water, or hot bricks, to the calves of the legs and to the feet.
> **General Observations.**—On restoration to life, a tea-spoon of warm water should be given; and then, if the power of swallowing be returned, small quantities of weak brandy and water, warm; the

them still in their forties and all of them relatively young, paid the ultimate price for the drinker's lifestyle.

I was referred to the gastroenterology department of the local hospital. First there was an ultrasound which established that, under all the layers of fat, I did have a liver. But there seemed to be an element of *The Hunt for Red October* about the proceedings. 'We know it's in there but we're not exactly sure where.'

The results of more exhaustive blood tests were conclusive. There was a worrying level of liver damage.

In anticipation of getting a hard time from the consultant, I had cut back on drinking for nearly a fortnight before my appointment. I lost about two pounds in weight.

I presented these facts, not in defence of my indefensible ways but in mitigation.

The consultant dismissed my claim that at least I was heading in the right direction. He did so with a wry smile on his face. He could smile. It wasn't his liver we were talking about.

He had a bedside manner which was cheerfully menacing. The consultant had examined my entrails and the divination was less than cheery. The levels of this, that and some other intestinal contaminants were quite worrying. My various internal organs had taken a bit of a doing.

The chief medicine man said any further ingestion of alcoholic beverages was not an option. After a long silence, I said surely the occasional glass of wine might be allowed.

He replied that in his long experience of treating journalists of my generation, moderation tended not to work. Only abstinence would do.

After a lengthier silence, I said: 'There will be redundancies in many sectors of the licensed trade.'

He replied, with that wry smile: 'I'll do my best to keep them going.'

I had finally been given the 'stop-drinking-or-you-will-die' ultimatum.

Too many of my colleagues, faced with this choice, had carried on drinking and had died . . . rather quickly.

I decided dying was not an option. For the first time since I was sixteen, alcohol was unequivocally off the menu.

2

Super tragic gastric illness, haemochromatosis . . .

In the course of my stop-drinking-or-die-soon cosy chat with the ghastly-enterologist, I had expected the word 'cirrhosis' to feature prominently. Cirrhosis, not work, is the scourge of the drinking class.

Thanks to the Internet, and with the help of Messrs Google and Wikipedia, we are all doctors these days. I was able to mug up on cirrhosis in advance of my appointment.

First, I checked for the signs and symptoms; I looked at my hands and was pretty sure I had the palmar erythema — 'Exaggerations of normal speckled mottling of the palm, due to altered sex hormone metabolism'.

I was not entirely sure I had Muehrcke's nails — 'paired horizontal bands separated by normal colour'.

I was more concerned about Dupuytren's contracture, the 'thickening and shortening of palmar fascia that leads to flexion

deformities of the fingers. Thought to be due to fibroblastic proliferation and disorderly collagen deposition. It is relatively common
(33% of patients).' There was definite evidence of this, or was it
just that I had always had fingers like thick sausages?

I had a feel of my man boobs for gynecomastia but could not
find much evidence of 'benign proliferation of glandular tissue
of male breasts presenting with a rubbery or firm mass extending
concentrically from the nipples.'

I looked downstairs for signs of hypogonadism; 'testicular atrophy
due to primary gonadal injury or suppression of hypothalamic or
pituitary function.' I was pretty certain my testicles had not shrunk
and, if anything, had gone up a few sizes. After purchasing a pair
of Calvin Klein latexy underpants, I had to ask the wife: 'Do my
balls look big in these?'

Whether my *cojones* had wasted or withered (other signs of
atrophy) was a matter for debate, or at least further research on
the Internet.

Certainly, for a man who had not been feeling himself, I had
been feeling a lot of myself lately.

Dr Wikipedia set a few alarm bells ringing with the information
about a complication of cirrhosis called hepatic encephalopathy.

This is where the liver does not clear ammonia and related nitrogenous substances from the blood. These are carried to the brain, affecting cerebral functioning with resultant neglect of personal appearance, unresponsiveness, forgetfulness, trouble concentrating, or changes in sleep habits.

'That's me,' I thought. 'Apart from the changes in sleep habits. I can always get to sleep, especially after a few pints.'

But that's the trouble with self-diagnosis on the Internet. It's a bit like wandering around the supermarket without a shopping list and ending up with a trolley full of stuff you don't need.

Surf your symptoms and you imagine afflictions you don't really have.

But, meanwhile, back in the real-life medical world, my consultant gastroenterologist had a theory that my liver damage was down to a condition called haemochromatosis.

It concentrates the mind wonderfully when you have something ending in -osis.

The clue to the possible haemochromatosis, the consultant said, was the high level of iron in my blood. The fact that I had type 2 diabetes was also significant.

The consultant said that having too much iron in the blood is as bad as having too little. With haemochromatosis — having too much — the body is unable to excrete iron. This may come as a

The Irish peasantry are in the habit of washing their faces with buttermilk as a cosmetic, and with great success. An excellent wash for freckles is made by scraping some horseradish very fine, and letting it stand for some hours in buttermilk, then straining, and using the wash night and morning.

Some persons prescribe citric acid, dissolved in water, of a strength sufficient to produce a slight pricking sensation. The juice of a lemon, squeezing into half a tumbler of water, is, however, a more certain means to effect the same result; or a little glycerine, mixed with elder-flower water, may be tried as a cosmetic wash. Any of these preparations, however, are useful, especially when assisted by the alteratives of magnesia, blue pill, and seidlitz powder.

To Remove Freckles.—Powdered nitre, moistened with water and applied to the face night and morning will soon remove freckles without injury to the skin.

Freckles.—To disperse them, take 1 oz. of lemon juice; ¼ dr. of powdered borax, and ½ dr. of sugar; mix, and let them stand a few days in a glass bottle till the liquor is fit for use; then rub it on the hands and face occasionally.

To Remove Freckles.—Dissolve, in ½ oz. of lemon juice, 1 oz. of Venice soap, and add ¼ oz. each of oil of bitter almonds, and deliquated oil of tartar. Place this mixture in the sun till it acquires the consistency of ointment. When in this state add three drops of the oil of rhodium, and keep it for use. Apply it to the face and hands in the manner following: Wash the parts at night with elder-flower water.

Freckles.—Take 1 oz. of lemon-juice, ¼ dr. of powdered borax and ½ dr. of sugar; mix, let them stand a few days in a glass bottle, then rub it on the hands and face occasionally. Or, mix two teaspoons of muriatic acid with 2 ozs. of spirits of wine; and 1½ pts. of distilled water. Or, 2 drs. of muriatic acid in 1 pt. of water, and a teaspoon of spirits of lavender. Apply with a camel hair pencil, or linen. Or, Horseradish steeped in sour milk for 12 hours, and a drop or two of tincture of myrrh. Wash two or three times per day.

A Cure for Freckles.—Scrape horseradish into a cup of cold sour milk; let it stand twelve hours, strain, and apply two or the times a day.

Another.—Mix lemon juice, 1 oz; powdered borax, ¼ dr.; sugar, ½ dr.; keep a few days in a glass bottle, then apply occasionally.

A Cure for Pimples.—Many of our young people are much troubled with an eruption upon the face. It often proves a great annoyance to them; but there is a simple remedy, which, if it does not effect a complete cure, will obviate the difficulty in a great degree, without the least injury to the health or skin.

To 1 gr. of corrosive sublimate add 1 oz. of rose water; filter, and apply twice a day.

Hands, to Whiten.—Take a wineglass of eau de Cologne, half a cup of lemon juice, scrape two cakes of Windsor soap to a powder; mix well, then add a teaspoon of sulphuric acid. Mould it, and let it harden.

COMPOUNDS TO PROMOTE THE GROWTH OF THE HAIR.—When the hair falls off, from diminished action of the scalp, preparations of cantharides often prove useful; they are sold under the names of Dupuytren's Pomade, Cazeuaze's Pomade, etc. The following directions are as good as any of the more complicated recipes:

surprise to those who felt at times they were excreting iron, but let us not go there.

The body dumps the iron into the heart, liver, pancreas and various other nooks and crannies. These deposits of iron bugger up (as the doctor *didn't* say) these important organs.

Haemochromatosis is hereditary, caused by two rogue genes. Blood tests would show whether or not I had it.

In the meantime, a regime of no alcohol, healthy eating and exercise was required.

The hospital doctor had explained haemochromatosis to me in layman's terms. I went home to my computer for Dr Wikipedia to tell me the full story.

First, I wanted to check out the hereditary bit. If it was in my genes, were my brothers and sisters, my children and grandchildren also at risk?

I read that the hereditary form of the disease is most common among those of Northern European ancestry, in particular those of Irish descent. My ancestors had come over to Scotland from Ireland sometime halfway through the nineteenth century.

I knew this because when I checked the surname Shields in a Scottish Tourist Board database, I was told I wasn't from these parts. This was a bit of a blow since I had considered myself tartan through and through.

I wrote an article about how I had been stripped of my Scottishness by a computer. The Irish Tourist Board, ever on the look-out for a bit of publicity, sent me copious details of my Irishness. I was a Shields, or *O'Sial* in Irish Gaelic, probably from Fermanagh or Tyrone.

My ancestors had been poets, philosophers and surgeons to the

Irish kings. So how come my more recent forebears had given up the poetry, philosophy and surgery in favour of digging ditches and pursuing other forms of manual labour in Scotland?

It was the potato famine, of course, which had dispersed so many Irish families all over the world, mainly North America. My ancestors only got as far as Glasgow and Dundee.

Hereditary haemochromatosis is called the Celtic Curse because it particularly affects people of Irish, Scots and Welsh origin.

I had always been team aware of my Celtic connections. I support Celtic, the famous Glasgow football team.

Someone who is fond, perhaps over-fond, of taking a drink is described as a man (or woman) of Celtic temperament. I think the euphemism applies to me.

Meanwhile, back in Dr Wikipedia's cyber surgery, I was checking on the genetics of the situation. It said:

Genetic studies suggest the original haemochromatosis mutation arose in a single person, possibly of Celtic ethnicity, who lived 60–70 generations ago. At that time when dietary iron may have been scarcer than today, the presence of the mutant allele may have provided a natural selection process reproductive advantage by maintaining higher iron levels in the blood.

Had I got the condition from an Irish ancestor sixty generations go? If so, had I passed this mutant 'allele' on to my children?

More urgently, I had to find out what an allele is. It turns out an allele is, 'an alternative form of a gene (one member of a pair) that is located at a specific position on a specific chromosome'. If this allele was dangerous, presumably there were modern treatments? Such as radiotherapy? Or 'nuke-allele' as it might be called.

If I had the rogue gene, I needed to know if I was heterozygous, which is a genetic donation from both parents, or homozygous, inheriting from just one.

If you are heterozygous, you have the full-blown disease. Without treatment you are heading for a lot of what Dr Wikipedia refers to ominously as 'end-organ damage'.

That could be liver cancer. One-third of people with cirrhosis and haemochromatosis develop liver cancer.

Or congestive heart failure. A build-up of excess iron in the heart interferes with its ability to pump blood.

'A number of problems can occur including death,' it states matter-of-factly. Then there is pigment change: 'Your skin may change colour to bronze or grey.' Faced with the choice, what are you going to say?

'I don't fancy grey. I'd prefer a kind of golden tan, but that's not an option so I'll have the bronze, please.'

Liver damage is seen as the badge of the alcohol abuser. Like legendary Scottish footballer Jim Baxter whose penchant for large quantities of rum saw him get through his own liver and two transplants.

By a cruel twist of fate, even the most religious and dedicated teetotaller can lose liver function through haemochromatosis. Although a Wee Free Presbyterian, or member of a similar strict sect, might have trouble explaining to the rest of the congregation that he hasn't touched a drop . . . honestly . . . and it is all the work of rogue genes.

Luckily, the condition is curable. But the only cure is to extract the excess iron by phlebotomy. Which is a posh medical name for blood-letting. A sufferer from haemochromatosis will have blood drained off, up to a pint a week initially, and then up to six times a year to keep the iron level down. Those who are homozygous do not need the phlebotomy but have to be careful not to ingest too much iron. Luckily, the gene tests showed that in terms of haemo-chromatosis I am not hetero but homo. Not the two rogue genes. Just one. Haufachromatosis.

To avoid taking in excess iron I assumed I would have to avoid spinach. I was ready for this sacrifice. But according to Dr Wiki-pedia, spinach contains ocalic and phytic acids which inhibit iron absorption. Go figure that one, Popeye!

I also have to limit the intake of vitamin C. When a bar person puts a slice of lemon in my sparkling water, I can ask: 'Are you trying to kill me?'

Only the occasional steak is allowed since red meat is high in iron. Sadly, seafood is also on the restricted list on the grounds that it brings a risk of food poisoning.

Alcohol also had to be limited. But since my gastroenteroligist had already ordered a total prohibition, this was not a problem.

So I faced my future of no alcohol, fewer prawns, and no slice of lemon in my Highland Spring with determination and even a feeling of release. As a reminder of my new life, I even have a song about it.

It goes, and you may want sing along:

Super tragic gastric illness, haemochromatosis
Even though the sound of it is something quite atrocious
If you keep off drink and stuff, it's not all that ferocious . . .

Sometimes I even do the accompanying wee jig like Dick van Dyke in the *Mary Poppins* movie.

3

My life as a teetotaller

With the words of the doctor ringing in my ears that the two choices were abstinence from alcohol or early death, I walked out of the hospital determined to follow the first option.

Fortunately, I have always been fond of water. When your mouth feels like the bottom of a budgie's cage (as it often does the morning after the night before) a glass of Adam's Ale is the very thing.

In my office I have a machine dispensing gloriously cool water from the Kinghill spa near Newmains in Lanarkshire. I should add that I work at home . . . alone. When I go for a water cooler moment I talk to myself.

Water is an essential part of the diet. Adults should drink between one and a half to three litres a day. Other beverages such as tea, coffee and fruit juices count towards the fluid target. Which means that, for many years, I was well over my water limit with lager and Guinness alone.

Inevitably, there is research which shows that over-consumption of water can be deleterious to the health. You could end up with hyponatraemia, also known as water intoxication. Your sodium and other body salts get too diluted, which causes dizziness and respiratory problems.

Perhaps some of those times I was dizzy after too many litres of lager, it wasn't the alcohol, it was the water intoxication that was to blame.

I estimate my daily water intake is nearly at the three-litre upper level. So far there have been no ill effects. There is the added benefit that you have to stop tapping away at your keyboard really often to go for a toilet break.

The word 'teetotal' has nothing to do with tea. There are various theories as to the origin of the word. One is that it was coined to emphasise the 'T' in total.

Another is that a chap with a stammer stood up at a temperance meeting and ended up extollong the virtues of 'tee-tee-tee-total abstinence'. I prefer the latter version.

So I drink tea. Being obsessive compulsive, it can't be just your Tetley or Nambarrie or even Twinings teabags. It's got to be green tea, oolong, jasmine or green with ginseng: all of which require hours of shopping at the Chinese supermarket.

Then there is rooibos, or red tea, the famed health-giving and caffeine-free brew from South Africa. It is the drink of the Khoi Khoi tribe but is now gathered on my behalf by my daughter

'A pint – and one for yourself'

Anna, the shopper, on hunting expeditions to Harvey Nichols.

My supplies of organic green jasmine, empress earl grey, snow flower early grey, bird of paradise, Xu Ya snowbuds white tea, and a fruity variety called strawberries and cream tea come not from the Far East but from the north-east of England. Kate from Darlington, mother of two of my grandchildren, introduced me to a company called Ringtons, which has made Geordieland the tea centre of the universe.

These speciality teas require to be treated with respect as part of a tea ceremony, just like in China or Japan. The Japanese ceremony, or *chaji*, can take up to four hours.

I have never managed to stretch making a cuppa last as long as that. But the process of choosing your variety of tea, selecting your tea cup, and listening to a bit of Radio 4 while the leaves infuse can keep you away from your work at the computer for up to half an hour. It's a Zen thing and cannot be rushed.

Another Zen pursuit is going to the pub. Even though you no longer drink alcohol, there is no reason why you should not still frequent your local for a spot of social interaction.

The first problem with being a teetotaller in a place devoted to the consumption of the hard stuff is choosing a soft drink. You will see the lost souls who are off the drink but really want a pint of Guinness or lager. They work their way balefully through a menu of Coca-Cola, Irn-Bru, orange juice, tomato juice, cranberry juice, tonic water, lemonade or fizzy water. Or bitter lemon, which is the bitterest pill of all.

My drink of choice was ginger beer. I could say I was popping down to the pub for a beer. There was also that happy childhood connection with Enid Blyton's *Famous Five* characters who consumed 'lashings of ginger beer' with their ham sandwiches.

Being of a diabetic disposition, I had to find diet ginger beer. Luckily, the Doublet Bar, one of my portfolio of preferred drinking establishments in Glasgow, sells diet Bundaberg which comes all the way from Australia. There is even a kangaroo on the label.

Bundaberg is a very acceptable ginger beer, just on the right side of fiery. With its heavy carbon footprint, the Aussie beverage also offers the opportunity for a bit of Roman Calvinist guilt, which is always a plus.

Ginger in Scotland is not just a soft drink made from the underground stem of the plant *Zingiber officinale*. It is also the generic term for what the Americans call 'soda' and the English call 'pop'.

So ginger can, in fact, be lemonade, cola, limeade, orangeade or — what was most delicious of all to my childhood palate — the rich vanilla flavour of American cream soda.

Using ginger as a generic term is a sign of working-class origins. Hence, the classic [i.e. ancient] story of a young man, unused to fine dining, who was attending a formal dinner. The first course involved a slice of melon. 'Would you like some ginger?' the waitress asked. Unaware of the practice of sprinkling some powdered ginger root on the melon, the lad replied: 'No, I'll just stick to the wine.'

A difficulty for the soft drinker in pubs is the perceived injustice of the price of non-alcoholic refreshments. Hard drinkers will fork out any amount of money for beer, wine and spirits. They may complain but they will pay up for their fix. But they will rail at the cost of a dash of cola to go with their rum.

My Bundaberg was coming in at a unit price of more than £5 a litre. I could buy equally good diet ginger beer from the supermarket for 20p a litre. In Zen mode, I do not complain. I realise that someone has to pay the money for the bar staff's minimum wage and the publican's flash Mercedes-Benz car.

As a soft drinker you spend less. A dedicated lager drinker, for instance, may consider a gallon or so a reasonable intake for a visit to the pub. One ginger beer and maybe a coffee will suffice for the teetotaller.

I discovered that you don't actually need bevvy to savour the essential ingredients of a visit to the pub. These are conversation, argument, debate and diatribe, not to mention gentle insult. The social interaction can actually be more enjoyable since the brain is not slightly deadened by alcohol.

There are times in the bar, of course, when there is little in the way of conversation, argument, debate, diatribe, and gentle insult ... just drunk people talking shite. In these circumstances, since you don't need to stay for a drink, you can make an excuse and leave.

Some publicans may not be too happy with customers who linger over a ginger beer or coffee. They will be worrying where their next Merc is coming.

There used to be a breed of Scottish bar owner who would take exception to customers who requested anything but the hardest of liquour. Ask for an orange juice and you might be told to 'feck off' to the nearest café.

In some establishments, suggest that you might like a slice of lemon in your gin and tonic and the response might be: 'This is a pub, not effen Malcolm Campbell's.'

Malcolm Campbell was a well-known chain of fruit and veg shops in the west of Scotland. 'Effen' is a mild and acceptable form of swearing as pioneered by Glasgow singer and songwriter Matt McGinn. Matt wrote a ditty about a beekeeper in the French town of Effen. But an 'effen bee' is Glasgow shorthand for something entirely different from a French honey-producing insect.

You can probably work out the semantics of 'effen bee'. 'Effen polis' is a phrase often used to describe the Glasgow constabulary.

Anyway, the new generation of publicans is more sophisticated and aware of its social duty to offer non-alcoholic beverages. They will happily sell you a Fairtrade skinny latté, fizzy water at the same price as lager, or ginger beer at a fiver a litre.

Being obsessively compulsive, I started to overdose on ginger, and not just the stuff in a bottle. A consultation with Dr Wikipedia revealed that root ginger is full of zingerone, shoals and gingerols, not to mention sesquiterpenoids, which all sound as if they might be very good for you. Ginger is also 'stappit fu' (which is Scottish for 'full') of vitamins and trace elements.

Ginger is said to be good for treating flu, coughs, colds, colic dyspepsia, nausea, seasickness and diarrhoea. It promotes a siala-gogue action, which, as you probably already knew, stimulates the production of saliva, making swallowing easier.

2. Injection for Chronic Diarrhea.—New milk, with thick mucilage of slippery elm, of each, 1 pt.; sweet oil, 1 gill; molasses, ½ pt.; salt, 1 oz.; laudanum, 1 dr. Mix, and inject what the bowels will retain.

Very many children, as well as grown persons, die annually of this disease, who might be saved by a proper use of the above injection and cordial. The injection should never be neglected, if there is the least danger apprehended.

Although I believe these would not fail in one case out of one hundred, yet I have some other prescriptions which are so highly spoken of, I will give a few more. The first, from Mr. Hendee, of Warsaw, Indiana, for curing Diarrhea, or Bloody Flux, as follows:

This king of spices is also credited with cholesterol-lowering properties but don't go there if you are already on warfarin for heart disease. Ginger may be useful for alleviating arthritic joint pain.

Research shows it may be helpful for treating diabetes, but mostly if you are a laboratory rat. A lump of root ginger can also be used as a suppository for constipated horses. You never know when this knowledge might come in handy.

A ginger infusion is reckoned to be even better than Barr's Irn-Bru, Scotland's national soft drink, for treating a hangover. Despite being a teetotaller, and therefore not requiring this cure, I took to having a pot of ginger tea, sweetened with honey or palm sugar, of a morning.

I also used lashings of ginger in my cooking. With onion and garlic, it makes a delicious base for all sorts of meat and chicken dishes. In Myanmar, shredded ginger is preserved in oil and mixed with nuts and seeds. In Malaysia, the ginger flower is added to salads and also sprinkled on soups.

The Japanese grate pickled ginger over their noodles and tofu. Being Scottish, I grated some into my porridge. It's interesting to spice up your oats but not as tasty as adding a good pinch of sea salt.

I could have called these memoirs *Ginger in My Porridge*, but Scottish author Angus Macvicar has already staked out that territory with *Salt in My Porridge*. As a journalist I have been careful to avoid plagiarism. I have also avoided clichés like the plague.

As with everything that's good to eat, ginger has been fingered by the health police. Scientists at the Ambrose Alli University in Nigeria conducted tests which proved that excess consumption of ginger had damaging effects on the livers of male adult rabbits. So 'ca canny' (which is Scottish for 'be careful') if you don't want to be an unwell bunny.

But back to My Life as a Teetotaller, which would in truth be a brief tale if I hadn't included all that stuff about publicans and their Mercedes motors, Effen polis and ginger in your porridge.

After getting the bad news from the doctor about the state of the liver, I embraced teetotalism with my usual obsessive-compulsive vigour. I wrote at some length about haemochromatosis and the need for temperance in a column in the *Sunday Herald*. I intoned gravely: 'If you spot me clutching a glass of strong drink, dash it from my lips and smite it from my hand.'

My article was bad news for at least one reader. He had been diagnosed with full-blown haemochromatosis but had omitted to tell his wife the bit about how he had to stop drinking. He was still having a regular 'swally', which is west of Scotland parlance for partaking of alcohol. She read what I had written and proceeded to dash strong drink from his lips and smite it from his hands.

I found the business of not drinking quite exhilarating. It was the best I had felt in forty years: alert, clear-headed and only slightly manic. I was getting thinner by the day, getting up with the lark and generally ready for a lark.

The onset of my abstinence coincided with an invitation to a gala gourmet dinner where the fine wines were flowing. Having a university degree whose subjects included beverage management (which was basically a year of wine-tasting), I was sorely tempted to increase my knowledge base by sampling the sumptuous vintages.

I managed to restrict myself to a token wetting of the lips, just to be polite. There was a more than token glug at the Turckheim Reserve *pinot gris* but only in deference to chef Albert Roux's superb terrine of foie gras, celeriac and lentils.

Then, throughout the festive season, which is a testing time, I still resisted temptation, apart from perhaps too liberal an application of brandy to the Christmas pudding.

In the years before I pursued abstemiousness, any time I drank ginger beer it was as a mixer for a large gin; usually as a thirst quencher in our notoriously hot Scottish summers. (Excess irony has always been my problem, even before the haemochromatosis.)

Like many a hard drinker turned soft, I tried to replicate the 'real' stuff. I searched for a non-alcoholic gin to perk up the ginger beer. I enquired at Demijohn on Byres Road in Glasgow, which describes itself as a 'liquid deli' and sells some very esoteric gins.

The staff were suitably mystified by my request for an alcohol-free version of mother's ruin.

But as the days progressed, I gradually moved out of the drinker's mindset. Not medicating myself with alcohol became the default position.

After only three months of my regime, a new set of blood tests brought amazing news. The doctor told me my liver results were normal, except from one indicator which was slightly elevated.

I did what any red-blooded Scotsman who had cleansed his blood of alcohol would do. I had a drink to celebrate.

It was just a carajillo de anis, a coffee with a dash of aniseed liqueur, a drink I had come to know and love in Barcelona. Then I had another. Then I was on two a day.

It started out with carajillo but soon I hit the harder stuff. I went on to the occasional cubata, another drink I had developed a fondness for in Barcelona. A cubata is whisky, rum, gin or brandy, topped up with Coca-Cola. They are alcopops for adults and are far too easy to drink.

I did get myself back on to coffee. Sadly, I discovered the espresso martini cocktail. Yes, there was coffee in it. But there was also vodka, Kahlua, brandy, Frangelico and triple sec.

It is an awesome concoction and was a delicious way for me to recommence the process of committing suicide by drink.

4

I'm not obese, I'm adipose with a net energy imbalance

On a visit to Disney's Animal Kingdom, I spent more time observing fat Americans than I did any of the other species on display. There was a definite feel-good factor as I watched the supersized natives devour burgers of dinosaur dimensions. They made me look thin. But in truth I was not that far behind in the corpulence stakes.

I remember being twenty-one years old and weighing in at about eleven stone. Next thing I knew, I was in my fifties and tipping the scales at 17st 4lbs. The standard measure of heftiness, the body mass index (BMI), confirmed that I was obese with a rating of 33.

There is a story about height ratios involving the legendary Irish rugby player Willie John McBride. He was on tour in Australia with the British Lions and, at a reception, was being chatted up by a local lady who complimented him on his fine 6ft 3ins physique. In that direct antipodean manner, the woman asked, gazing downwards: 'Tell me, are you built in proportion?' She was not thinking about his BMI but about one part of his anatomy in particular.

'No,' said Willie John modestly, 'If I was in proportion, I would be six foot eight tall.'

In my case, if I were to be in proportion (in BMI terms and not what that Aussie lady was thinking about) I would have to be 6ft 4ins to qualify as 'merely overweight'. To be normal I would need to stand 7 feet tall.

So, ideally, I should put on some height. I am 5ft 10ins which is not small but I am only 29 inches in the inside leg. I have a theory there was a mix-up somewhere along the line and I ended up with a pair of legs that should have gone to a very short-arsed person.

There are various ways to try to increase your height. You can take growth hormone injections. You can have your legs broken and bits of bone added. Both courses of action appear problematic.

Or you can opt for the totally safe miracle method as advertised on the www.gainheight.com website. You can be four inches taller in 'just three short months' by wearing a pair of insoles. These are no ordinary insoles.

They are the YOKO Japanese insoles which are made of green rubber and have knobbly bits. They massage your feet reflexologically and stimulate the pituitary gland, which promotes growth. The YOKO people (no relation to Mrs Lennon) say you can add two inches to your spine and another two inches to your legs.

I am sceptical of these claims. But I am sure that if you stuff a pair of green knobbly insoles that are about one centimetre thick into your shoes, you will definitely gain height. Probably about one centimetre.

> ITCHING FEET FROM FROST-BITES.—To Cure. — Take hydrochloric acid, 1 oz.; rain water, 7 ozs.; wash the feet with it 2 or 3 times daily, or wet the socks with the preparation. until relieved.
> A gentleman whose feet had been frozen. in the Alps. eight years before, and another man's had been frozen two years before, on the Sierra Nevada Mountains, were effectually cured by its use.

I have managed to rationalise my excessive weight by claiming to be big-boned. After all, there are many parts of my body which are entirely normal. People tell me I have a fine pair of legs, for instance.

It is in the waist department where I fail to meet requirements. I have many great-nephews and nieces who have given me an affectionate nickname. They have abbreviated Great Uncle Tom to 'GUT'. Sadly, it is all too appropriate.

I remember when I used to buy my trousers at Marks & Spencer off the 30-inch waist rail. Then my belly started to have a life of its own.

At the apex of my bigness, I had gone up to 42 inches. A pair of 42-inch waist trousers with 29-inch leg looks awfully like those worn by circus clowns.

Over the years, this gradual increase in my M&S-waist-to-inside-leg ratio has been a source of embarrassment and shame, but not shameful enough over those years for me to do anything about it.

My dietician, helpfully supplied by the National Health Service as part of my treatment for type 2 diabetes, said bluntly that all my health problems were down to that big layer of fat round my middle.

I hastened to Dr Wikipedia for a second opinion and more information. I learnt that abdominal fat just doesn't sit there. It is especially active, secreting a group of hormones called adipokines that may impair glucose tolerance. So I added adipokines to the long list of words I didn't understand but which were conspiring to kill me.

Impaired glucose tolerance does not sound all that bad until you get to the bit where it increases morbidity. That's not morbidity where you think: 'I'm feeling a bit gloomy today'; it's morbidity as in the probability of catching a serious illness and dying.

Whilst consulting Dr Wikipedia, I discovered that I need not describe myself as obese. Obesity, after all, is for trailer trash and folk who live in sink housing estates. Not for professional classes in the boho chic, west end of Glasgow.

'A 32" waist you say?'

I was pleased to discover that I actually suffer from central adiposity caused by a net energy imbalance. This was part of some metabolic syndrome.

Metabolic syndrome was first mooted in 1947 by a Marseilles physician called Dr Jean Vague. Now, Vague is not a very reassuring name for a doctor. But Dr Vague was pretty sure that upper body obesity predisposed people to diabetes, atherosclerosis, gout and calculi. That is calculi as in stones that form from mineral salts in bodily organs and cause all sorts of problems. Not calculus; that

fiendishly difficult maths subject which ruined your schooldays.

Metabolic syndrome can also come with hyperlipoproteinemia, hyperuricemia and hepatic steatosis. I didn't check these guys out because, at that point, I had kind of overdosed on Internet hypochondria and I was getting a bit worried.

But, hey, it was good to have a syndrome to blame when in reality your central adiposity is a fat belly. And the net energy imbalance is actually eating and drinking too much and doing no exercise.

Whether you are obese or suffer from central adiposity, the end result is the same. Doctors from the American Heart Association (who know a bit about the subject) say that: 'after adjustment for all the standard cardiovascular risk factors, sagittal abdominal diameter — a measure of abdominal fat — is significantly associated with increased risk of sudden death.'

I decided that my dietician and the American Heart Association were probably right. I had to go on a regime. I should constantly measure my weight, my BMI and my waist-to-hip ratio.

But the most obvious improvement I could make to my health was to achieve a significant decrease in my trouser size. As Shakira, the Colombian chanteuse, nearly said: the waist don't lie.

5

Diabetes is diabolic, intit?

First, I should explain 'diabolic, intit?' It comes from a poem by Bud Neill, cartoonist and master of Glasgow demotic. Demotic describes how people really speak. Bud's verse is as follows:

> Winter's come the snow has fell
> Wee Josie's nose is froze as well
> Wee Josie's frozen nose is skintit
> Winter's diabolic, intit?

Wee Josie's frozen nose has nothing to do with diabetes. I just thought I would try and cheer you up before getting into a topic which is truly diabolic and dark and gruesome and with little scope for light relief.

Diabetes is known as the silent killer. It can be working away insidiously for years on your system before you know you have got it.

I discovered I had type 2 diabetes purely by chance. It was diagnosed by my brother John, the really clever brother who is not a doctor but should have been.

John suffers from the condition. Part of his treatment involves using a wee electronic machine to measure blood-sugar levels. With evangelistic zeal, he was testing family and friends for type 2 diabetes.

One small prick of a finger later, the machine revealed my blood sugar level was 22. It should be no more than 10 after a meal, or between four and six if you haven't eaten.

> **A DIABETES.**—Drink wine, boiled with ginger, as much and as often as your strength will bear. Let your drink be milk and water. All milk meats are good; or, drink three or four times a day a quarter of a pint of alum posset, putting 3 drs. of alum to 4 pts. of milk. It seldom fails to cure in eight or ten days; or, infuse ½ oz. of cantharides in a pint of elixir of vitriol. Give from ten to thirty drops in Bristol water twice or thrice a day.

Brother John said this was quite worrying and referred me to a doctor, one who unlike him had been lucky enough to get to medical school. Diabetes? That ailment which means you can't eat too many sweeties and you might have to give yourself an insulin jag. I could not recall many people I knew who had died of diabetes. I filed brother John's diagnosis in the non-urgent category.

Some months later, I had an appointment with my GP and I mentioned, but only in passing, the test carried out by my brother not the doctor. The GP took some blood for testing. Not just a drop from a finger, but enough to fill three or four phials. 'Nearly a whole armful,' as Tony Hancock protested in his comedy sketch, *The Blood Donor*.

My blood-sugar levels, the tests revealed, were worryingly high and I most likely had type 2 diabetes. The GP was reassuring. The condition can be managed by lifestyle management or, failing that, medication.

Of course, I hastened to the Internet for a consultation with Dr Wikipedia. It turned out that, with diabetes, I had got another syndrome. And not just an ordinary syndrome but one that came with disordered metabolism.

Its full name is diabetes mellitus. Mellitus is not to be confused with my happy condition 'Melitis', which comes from being married to a woman called Melanie, or Mel for short.

Diabetes mellitus occurs when the body is unable to convert glucose in the blood into energy as it should. This conversion should be done by the hormone insulin which is produced by your pancreas.

The pancreas is a small organ tucked below your stomach and should not be confused with St Pancras, the lovely old railway station in London which has been converted into the terminal for trains to Paris. St Pancras has the longest champagne bar in Europe, possibly the world, which is ideal for a *Brief Encounter* but may not be good news for the pancreas.

Type 1 diabetes is when there is a basic fault with the pancreas which fails to produce insulin. It is lethal unless insulin is put into the body, usually by injection. Type 2 grows on you, usually as a result of a lifestyle of too much weight and inactivity.

It is described as 'adult onset', but younger generations, who have embraced obesity as a way of life, are developing the condition in greater numbers.

With type 2, the pancreas is producing insulin but the body is unable to use it properly. This is called insulin resistance.

.**14.** **Tobacco Eye Water.**—Fine cut tobacco the size of a common hickory nut; sugar of lead equal in bulk; rain water, 2 ozs.; opium the size of a pea. Reduce it with more water if necessary.

I had perceived type 2 as the more cuddly version of diabetes. That was before Dr Wikipedia introduced me to some new words that might kill me, or at least cause considerable collateral damage.

These included atherosclerosis (which I already knew about, but vaguely) and a terrible trio called nephropathy, retinopathy and neuropathy. Atherosclerosis is hardening of the arteries. Nephropathy is kidney disease. Retinopathy is an eye disease. Neuropathy is a degeneration of the nervous system.

I now knew why my GP, while remaining calmly reassuring that the type 2 diabetes could be controlled, had set up a raft of appointments with a gastroenterologist, an optometrist, a podiatrist and a dietician.

When consulting Dr Wikipedia, the eye is naturally drawn to the worst-case scenarios. With atherosclerosis and his three 'pathy' companions Nephro, Retino and Neuro, the worst involves heart attack, stroke, kidney failure, blindness and LEA.

LEA looks quite an innocent acronym until you spell it out: lower extremity amputation.

6

An Me Wi a Bad Leg Tae

'Complications' is the nice, unthreatening word the doctors use to describe the heart failure, blindness et al, which can accompany diabetes if the worst comes to the worst. 'Sorry, there's a wee complication. We have to perform a lower extremity amputation. I'm afraid you'll be a foot shorter.'

That would be just my luck. Bad legs run in my family.

Like my father's war wound. He sustained his injury while walking home through the Gorbals during the blackout after his shift as a tram driver. In the pitch dark, he clattered into the sharp edges of a metal milk-delivery barrow which had been left on the pavement by some fool. My father, Charlie, was not a man for swear words and actually used the word 'fool' to describe the person who had left the barrow in ambush.

Probably because it was wartime and there were others with more serious wounds to be treated, my father did not get it treated properly and had an ulcer in his shin which never seemed to get better.

He was always having to put acroflavin on it. For some reason this name 'acroflavin' sticks in my mind, as does the memory of watching my father spreading the greeny-yellow cream on to gauze pads to put on his leg that would not heal.

My maternal grandfather, a wee Hebridean, had a leg cut off but I'll tell you more about that in the chapter on gout. My mother was a martyr to her feet but I'll save the details for the bit about how there never seemed to be enough fish for tea.

Before getting down to the business of the gruesome foot and leg ailments which can befall the diabetic, I should explain the title of this chapter.

An Me Wi a Bad Leg Tae is a play by Billy Connolly, a Glasgow-born comedian. The play is not about complications of the lower extremity. It is a vehicle for the rich patois of his native city for which Mr Connolly has a very good ear.

Billy, or the Big Yin as he was known in a previous life, worked in the Glasgow shipbuilding yards where Glasgow's unique style of humour was forged. The style of humour was probably also forged in forges, of which the city had many, as well as large engineering factories. But the shipyard workers seem to have cornered the credit.

The Big Yin might also have written a play specifically about industrial ailments. It could have been called *An Me Wi a Broken Flask Tae*. Legend has it that a favourite excuse for a Clydeside worker to have a 'duvet day' (before there were duvets) was that the vacuum container for his day's ration of tea was defective.

Now for some cheery statistics.

DFUs precede 85% of non-traumatic LEAs. A DFU is a diabetic foot ulcer. You know what an LEA is. 'Non-traumatic' does not mean you won't be upset by losing your foot. It means the amputation did not happen due to an accident.

In the USA, there are twenty million people with diabetes. Five million of them will develop foot problems. Up to half a million will undergo foot or leg amputations.

The number of diabetes-related amputations in Australia is approximately 3,400 per year.

You will understand why, when I go to my diabetes clinic, I listen very carefully to the podiatrist, or foot man.

4. Dr. Hariman's Innocent and Sure Cure for Corns, Warts and Chilblains.—Nitric and muriatic acids, blue vitriol, and salts of tartar, of each 1 oz. ; add the blue vitriol, pulverized, to either of the acids, and in the same way add the salts of tartar; when done foaming, add the other acid, and in a fews days it will be fit for use.

DIRECTIONS.—For frosted feet, rub them with a swab or brush, wet with this solution very lightly, every part that is red and dry; in a day or two, if not cured, apply again as before. For corns, apply in like manner, scraping off dead skin before using. For warts, wet once a week until they disappear, which will be soon, for it is a certain cure in all the above cases, and very cheap. So says the Doctor, of Anderson, Ind.

5. A gentleman in Ohio offers to pay ten dollars apiece for all corns not cured in three days by binding a bit of cotton batting upon it, and wetting it three times a day with spirits of turpentine.

6. I am assured by a gentleman of Syracuse, N. Y., that a plaster of the "Green Mountain Salve," put upon a corn, will completely cure it by the time it naturally comes off.

I got some of these statistics from the *Diabetic Foot Journal*, one of the many medical publications I now subscribe to via the Internet. For a more general view of ill-health, I recommend *Morbidity and Mortality Weekly Report*. This will keep you hypochondriacally up to speed on a whole range of diseases.

> **GANGRENE.**—The partial death of a part; the preliminary stage to mortification, or the absolute death of a part.
> The CAUSES of gangrene are very numerous. It may arise from any excessive inflammatory action, from extreme cold, great bodily prostration, from severe blows, wounds, and accidents, and, indeed, from any cause that greatly depresses the vital powers; it also arises spontaneously in persons advanced in life, showing itself in the feet or toes, and, among the aged peasantry, is a very frequent cause of death.

But don't go to ReverseGangrene.com. You won't like it. It tells you much more than you would ever want to know about gangrenous feet, with pictures of black, dead flesh where toes used to be.

There used to be a DJ on Radio Clyde called Frank Skerrett who played brilliant songs from the 1950s. Songs like the 'Old Rugged Cross' and 'Nobody's Child' that were deep-rooted in the West of Scotland psyche. Frank had a highly developed sense of humour.

One night, he told his listeners that he had been in hospital to have a few toes amputated. It may well have been an LEA because of a DFU because Frank looked as if he enjoyed the kind of life-style that takes you there. He signed off his programme that night with 'Toot Toot Tootsie! (Goodbye).'

Most diabetic foot ulcers develop without the sufferer knowing. They can be caused by something as simple as an ingrown toenail or even blisters from ill-fitting shoes.

The patient may not feel the discomfort because of the neuropathy which deadens the nerve endings. The poor circulation of blood, as a result of the atherosclerosis, means the wound may not heal.

Which brings us, unfortunately, to gangrene; craters of foul-smelling, dead and dying flesh.

One of the things I wish I didn't know about gangrene is that it comes in two varieties: wet and dry. They are both pretty nasty. The photos on ReverseGangrene.com would give you the boke.

The boke (sometimes spelt 'boak') is a Scottish word for the initial stages of the process of vomiting. Strangely enough, there is also a variety called the dry boke.

There is an ice cream manufacturer in Pickering, North Yorkshire, by the name of Boak. 'Try Boak's delicious ices' is their slogan. It is a source of amusement to Scottish tourists who find their way to North Yorkshire.

The surgeons will not cut off your gangrenous foot willy-nilly. They will first attempt some debridement.

Debridement sounds like some medieval ritual practised by the lord of the manor, in the manner of *droit de seigneur*. But it is just a nicer word for cutting off what doctors call non-viable flesh.

If you're unfortunate enough to have a suppurating foot ulcer, you won't have to tell your friends you're going to hospital to get your gangrene scraped. Just say you're off to your physician for a spot of debridement.

Some doctors still use an ancient treatment for gangrene. They will let loose an army of maggots on the affected area. Like any army, this army of maggots marches on its stomach. There is nothing a maggot likes better for lunch than some putrid flesh.

The idea of a group of maggots gathering for a convivial lunch at a diabetic foot ulcer is disgusting; unless you're a maggot. But it is an image I find useful.

I have a terrible weakness for a Scottish delicacy called the macaroon bar. It is a piece of confectionary whose innards appear to consist entirely of icing sugar. Potato is used as a bulking agent but Ma Broon in her cookbook stipulates that the macaroon bar must not be tattie-flavoured. Add extra sugar until there is no taste of the tuber.

The sweet, doughy mixture is then dipped in melted chocolate and covered in toasted desiccated coconut. For me, it's an addiction. One macaroon bar is one too many and a thousand's not enough.

I developed my macaroon habit while going to the football as a boy. In the 1950s and 1960s, before all-seated stadia with fast-food outlets, there were independent entrepreneurial food retailers who would mingle with the crowds on the terracings.

For some reason, they only ever had two items on sale: macaroon bars and chewing gum. There may have been some ancient Glasgow by-law which restricted the pedlars to this duo of sweetmeats. It is a tradition long gone and its origin is lost in antiquity, which means I searched the Internet for a suitable explanation but couldn't find one.

The terracing salesmen would announce their presence with the cry: 'Erra macaroon bars and the spearmint gum.'

'Erra' is local dialect for 'here are'. It was used in much the same way that Spanish tapas bars have signs saying *'Hay ostras'* or *'Hay croquetas de bacalao'* indicating the availability of oysters or croquettes of salt cod.

I once saw a blackboard outside an English pub in Benidorm which announced, 'Hay Hula-hoops'.

I was going to tell you about how I once worked with Ma Broon on the *Sunday Post*. Well, she was the star of *The Broons* cartoon strip and I was a humble reporter. But if I start on the subject of the *Sunday Post*, it would be too long a digression and I would never get back to the subject of gangrene.

In my diabetic condition, I can no longer afford to gorge on macaroon bars. If I did, the blood sugar would reach danger levels. I would get the neuropathy and the atherosclerosis right bad. I

> **Wounds—Putrid.**—Wash them morning and evening with warm decoction of agrimony. If they heal too soon, and a matter gathers underneath, apply a poultice of the leaves pounded, changing them once a day till well. Or, apply a carrot poultice; but if a gangrene comes on, apply a wheat flour poultice (after it has been by the fire till 't begins to ferment) nearly cold. It will not fail.

might have a gangrenous lump instead of a big toe. I would be in for debridement or worse.

So when I look at a macaroon bar now I don't see a delicious morsel. I have a vision of maggots eating my foot.

This lifestyle management device works in much the same way as putting a photo of your fat self on the fridge door.

My loved ones still give me macaroon bars at Christmas and on birthdays. I suppose I could ask them to get diabetic chocolate instead. But the handbook *Diabetes for Beginners* says: 'Don't be tempted by diabetic foods. They offer no benefit to people with diabetes. They are expensive, just as high in fat and calories, have a laxative effect and still affect your blood glucose levels.'

There are obviously a few bucks to be made out of diabetes. It turns out the folk down at ReverseGangrene.com have a treatment for gangrenous diabetic foot ulcers. It is called 'nutritional revascularization'. This stimulus of blood flow is achieved by a health drink called Clear-G Formula which offers 'optimized limb salvage'.

Clear-G Formula contains ninety-seven natural ingredients. These include all the vitamins under the sun. It has iodine, magnesium, vanadium, boron, potassium, zinc, manganese and many other elements.

It also contains extracts of apple, grapefruit, turmeric, horse chestnut seed, cranberry, grape seed, olive leaf, green tea, marigold,

Swedish bilberry, milk thistle, Japanese giant knotweed, bitter melon leaf, witch hazel leaf, Jerusalem artichoke, aloe vera, beetroot and carrot.

With all this stuff in it, Clear-G costs US $200 for a twenty-one-day treatment. This may sound like spending an arm and a leg in the hope of saving a foot or a leg. ReverseGangrene.com offers testimonials, some referring to Clear-G as 'a miracle'. Mind you, at the foot of the list of ingredients, it states: 'This product is not intended to diagnose, treat, cure or prevent any disease.'

Instead of macaroon for Christmas, I hope for a few pairs of diabetic socks. These are socks made to control moisture, which can reduce the risk of infection. They are made without seams or wrinkle-prone material to reduce pressure and blistering. They have 'non-binding' loose tops which constrict less and improve blood flow.

Socks can be a factor in good health. Former Prime Minister James Callaghan attributed his living to a grand old age to the fact that he always sat down to put his socks on.

I used to treat my feet in a cavalier fashion, even ignoring outbreaks of athlete's foot. I didn't even dry between my toes. Apparently Glaswegians are remiss at towelling between the lower digits while up in Aberdeen, they are quite religious about it. Mind you, it was a Neep (a North-Eastern Ethnic Person) who propounded this theory.

Now, my podiatrist would be proud of me. Every little piggy gets individual attention. I am very attached to my toes and I want it to stay that way.

I am no heel when it comes to looking after the sole. I often have a look at them in a mirror. I have regular foot massages. My lower extremities are creamed and sprayed to within an inch of their hopefully long lives.

The Spanish for feet is *pies*. When a Scottish pub in Benidorm puts out a blackboard advertising the availability of *pies* the Spaniards think it mean's pig's feet, a local delicacy, for lunch.

7

In the name of the wee man

Old age does not come alone. It is accompanied by gradual, and not so gradual, changes to the body. There are the joints that remain stiff no matter how assiduously they are internally oiled with patent remedies. There are other bits that only become suitably stiff with the help of wee blue pills. Or yellow pills if you prefer Cialis to Viagra.

Among other corporeal conundra, there is the question of whether the head has got bigger or the hair has shrunk. Whatever, they no longer fit each other.

More worrying for me was a disparity which had occurred in the downstairs department.

You will notice the euphemism 'downstairs department'. It's my *Sunday Post* training from forty years ago. In a story headed 'Tight trousers may impair your chances of fatherhood' young people were warned of the dangers of wearing breeks that were 'too tight at the fork.' Crotch or groin were presumably considered a bit too graphic for the newspaper's douce readers.

Anyway, back in my downstairs, there was that bit of skin which we will call the foreskin since this is not the *Sunday Post*. It had become like a wee jumper that had got much tighter and was more difficult to pull over the head.

Not the head up top that was going bald. The head down there with the policeman's helmet. I'm talking about a problem of unretractability which, fortunately, was treatable through the NHS. Unfortunately, the treatment involved the surgeon's knife.

Circumcision, I can tell you, is not a prospect to be viewed lightly in later life. Shakespeare had it right when he said in *Hamlet*, Act two, Scene two: 'There is a divinity which shapes our ends, rough-hew them how we will.'

A friend who underwent the procedure as a late forty-something testified to the potential for pain. He had to go through the whole thing twice when his stitches burst the first time round. As he put it, graphically but inaccurately: 'The surgeon made a see you enn tee of it.' That would be another operation entirely.

As I sit here writing this, I see the word 'tools' among the menu options on my laptop screen. It seems entirely appropriate in this scenario. As does the fact that the name of the manufacturers of the computer application consists of the words 'micro' and 'soft.'

The surgeon offered various tool options that stopped short of a full circumcision. There is the dorsal slit, which relieves the tightness of the wee jumper but leaves it flapping loose and untidily

> **How to Make a Horse Stand to be Castrated.**—Put chloroform on a sponge and hold it to his nose a few seconds until he closes his eyes; remove it, and alter him. This can be given to perform any operation—you can buy it at the drug store for seventy-five cents per pound.

like an old fella's cardigan; dog-eared, like a pair of spaniel's lugs, to mix another simile.

The ventral slit is a vent on the obverse side which is neater, transforming the jumper from a tight crew-neck to a comfier V-neck. Then there is the preferred option, the prepuce-plasty where the neck is given a nick here and there and re-sewn across the way to give a more off-the-shoulder effect. Kind of Giorgio Yourmanny.

In the immediate post-operative state, Yourmanny looked a bit like Miss Piggy but not so cute. Pinky but not very perky. It could have got me a job in a freak show. Or a gig at the Edinburgh Festival Fringe as an alternative to *Puppetry of the Penis* or *The Vagina Monologues*.

When the wounds healed, it stopped looking so much like Miss Piggy. It is no George Clooney but it is comfy which is what matters.

What I did not suspect when I was being done, was that I was suffering from phimosis as a side effect of type 2 diabetes. At least that is what I deduce from consulting my colleague Dr Wikipedia.

I regret not knowing I had this condition. When people asked how I was keeping, I could have said: 'Fine, apart from a wee touch of phimosis. It's from the Greek *phimos*, meaning muzzle.'

Then, the next time we met, they might ask: 'How's your muzzle the day?'

The condition is available in many degrees of discomfort and unattractiveness. I was glad to have just this wee touch of phimosis and not the banalitis xerotica bitterns (BXO) version with its atrophic white patches on the affected area. Although the other effect of BXO, the whitish ring of indurated (hardened) tissue which usually forms near the tip might have given the wee man the aspect of a clergyman.

I have no complaints about my NHS makeover in the downstairs department. But there is an action group which is firmly against surgeons taking the knife to phimosis.

It is called Norm-UK, which seems an anonymous kind of name. But what were they gonna call it? The Campaign against Mutilation of the Penis, or something else equally blunt (or do I mean pointed)?

You will know the Jewish story about the mohel, the man who performs circumcisions. In the front window of his premises, he has a display of clocks. 'Why clocks?' he is asked. 'What should I put in my window,' he replies.

We will not reprise the story about the mohel who gets a retirement present of a wallet made out of foreskins. Okay ... when rubbed, it became a suitcase.

The people at Norm-UK probably do not appreciate jokes about

Sigh!

circumcision. With the possible exception of Alan Cumming, the Glasgow actor par excellence, who is a patron of the charity.

Norm-UK recommends a few treatments short of the knife. For the slightly more tractable cases, stretching techniques can be useful. This involves the application of baby oil and Vaseline and manipulating the affected area for a few minutes at least twice a day. Catholics may have to tell the priest all about it later in the confessional.

Steroid creams should be used if there is no progress after a month's manipulation. The creams have to be massaged inside and out three times a day. If anyone asks: 'How's the phimosis?' you can say: 'It's coming along. The wee man is on steroids.'

The Norm-UK website contains suggestions as to how the effects of a circumcision may be mitigated if not exactly reversed. This is no easy task and involves some innovative devices.

There is the TLC Tugger, a conical device which is attached to the skin left on the member and used, as far as I could make out from not looking too closely at the photos, to lift weights.

There is the PUD, the Penile Uncircumcising Device. This is a lump of stainless steel (imagine the wee man as Metal Mickey) which is attached and gravity does the stretching. Loose-fitting clothing is recommended to avoid giving the impression the wearer has a gun in his pocket.

There are various other devices such as the Foreballs and the Glansie, mostly made of steel. The Senslip is made of rubber. It is a wee (or large, depending on size) jersey which fits snugly over the circumcised mannie. It's a pity it couldn't be called the Ganzie.

On a serious note, it should be said that Norm-UK campaigns against unnecessary circumcision, wherever it is practised in the world.

8

Mother's milk and mother's mince

To the long list of ailments in this book, I could have added pneumonia, chicken pox, diphtheria, whooping cough, measles and mumps. According to family legend, I was a sickly infant and by the age of two had already gone through most of the available childhood illnesses.

I was skinny and feeble and when I was just a year old there were fears for my survival. My mother had to fatten me up. I was given the cream from the top of the milk.

I was obviously fond of milk. According to reports, I insisted on being breastfed well beyond the normal age. My mother said: 'Aye, oor Tommy liked a wee drink after his mince and tatties.'

You've got to keep your strength up. All that toddling can be tiring.

I don't know how old I was when I was still suckling away but apparently I could hold a decent conversation between mouthfuls.

I do know that I was *not* fed mother's milk through the railings at school, so my attachment to the mammary was not as enduring as some.

The early feeding habits may be responsible for the fact that, like many males, I have had a passing interest in breasts from a young age. But it was also a clever move on my part.

Studies of breastfed children, as reported in the *Proceedings of the National Academy of Sciences*, confirm that mother's milk may be a factor in higher IQ levels in later life. The breast milk can add seven IQ points.

This maybe helped me to pass my 'quali' and get into the Latin class when I moved from St Robert's primary to the big school. Both the quali and Latin have been consigned to the dustbin of educational history.

The big school was called Bellarmine and was supposed to offer a brave new comprehensive vision. In fact, it operated a ruthless educational apartheid.

With my mother's milk IQ, I was put in the so-called top section to recite *amabam, amabas, amabat*. Which Latin scholars will recognise as the singular forms of the past imperfect conjugation of the verb 'to love'. I thought then, and still think now, *amabam* sounded like Glaswegian for 'I am a bit of an idiot'. *Amabas* could have been a bit of gang graffiti. *Amabat* meant you were a small furry flying creature.

Meanwhile, down the educational food chain, my pals were doing useful things like woodwork and helping the jannie.

The subject of this chapter is supposed to be nutrition not education, so let us hasten back to the early 1950s and the kitchen table in Brock Road in Glasgow's Househillwood council housing estate, where the Shields, seven children and two parents, gather to dine. Or 'have your tea', as we called it.

I must have taken kindly to my mother's fattening-up regime. My nickname was 'little Tommy Tucker', after the nursery rhyme about a chap who sang for his supper.

I had become a sturdy wee fellow. Maybe a bit too sturdy since my other nickname was 'the wee fat pea'. It seems my life was pea-shaped long before it went pear-shaped.

There was the conundrum of mother's mince on Tuesdays. Her Monday stovies, a stew of sausages, potato and onions, were rich and unctuous. But her mince was often watery and not entirely bursting with flavour.

In later years, faced with an unsatisfactory plate of mince in a canteen or restaurant, I would say to the staff that it was just like my mother used to make. They did not know it was a complaint not a compliment.

But it turns out my mother was battling against all the odds when it came to mince. She got good quality minced beef out of Galloway's the butchers.

Her problem was that my older siblings would come home from work or school, declare themselves hungry and dip a slice of bread into the pot of bubbling mince to keep the wolf from the door.

Some siblings, and they know who they are, dipped in more than one slice of bread. 'Eat the Breid', as one sibling became known, would often dip an outsider or two. And it wasn't just gravy but lumps of mince he was after.

The result was that mother had to add extra water to replenish the pot. Despite the addition of an extra Oxo cube, the mince did not recover from the depredations. Another part of the ritual was that mother put a whole onion into her mince and this was served in its entirety on my father's plate. Not even 'Eat the Breid' managed to get any of it.

The meat filling in the Co-op mince rounds that we had on Wednesdays was much richer and more savoury than mother's efforts. A mince round is a pie filled with mince and is the subject of a good joke by Chic Murray, Scotland's master of comic surrealism. A bloke goes into the butcher's and asks if he can have a mince round. The butcher says, 'Of course, just carry on.'

It's the way Chic tells them and when he told that one, he would walk a bit light on his loafers. But it's not very PC these days to talk about light on the loafers and mincing around, so we won't go there.

Strangely, mince, which can be the food of the gods if 'Eat the Breid' hasn't siphoned off all the flavour, is a word used in Scotland to describe something of low quality.

A well-known US singer famously changed his name to The Artist formerly known as Prince. Shortly afterwards it was rumoured that Sydney Devine, a popular Scottish balladeer, wished to be known thenceforth as The Singer formerly known as Mince.

Mother's mince was mince but her soups were magnificent. They were rich and thick and stuck to your ribs. The Scotch broth was bursting with glutinous barley, the lentil soup lumpy with carrot and potato.

The eating was enhanced by the fact you had helped make the soups. Hours, it seemed, were spent grating the carrots and turnips. You were allowed to grate the veg down to the smallest size, at great risk to the tips of your fingers, but were kept well away from the sharp knives.

The Scotch broth did two courses. First, as a hot soup with lumps of plain bread. Plain bread was thick and doughy, compared to a more refined and expensive variety which was called 'pan'. People who affected poshness or tried to get above their station were described as 'pan loaf'.

The meat which had been used to flavour the soup — flank of mutton or beef for the Scotch broth and ham for the lentil soup — would be divided up and served back in the soup plate as a main course with plenty of potatoes and usually some cabbage.

When I'm in an expensive restaurant which serves its food country-style and I get my main course in a soup plate, I think of how authentically rustic a chef my mother was and she didn't even know it.

To this day I retain a great liking for cabbage. Slow-cooked in a sealed pan with a knob of butter and loads of pepper; as choucroute in the Alsace style, topped with various cuts of pork for one person, which would have kept the Shields going for a week; or spicy South Indian style.

With just the seven children, the Shields of Brock Road was one of the medium-sized family units down our way. The Bentleys and the Youngs were well into double figures.

Children of the larger families would joke that at mealtimes, it was a case of SOS: stretch or starve. In our house, the phrase 'I'm starving' was usually met with the response from my father: 'You don't know what starving means.'

I had assumed that this was a reference to children in Africa. Or 'black babies' as we called them. We had collections for the black babies in St Robert's primary. Your ma gave you a penny and you put it in the tin for the black babies. Sometimes, you didn't put it in the tin and spent it on a McCowan's penny dainty.

This lump of toffee inevitably left a bad taste in the mouth. A black baby was going hungry. And you had just committed a sin, probably mortal and would go to the bad fire. Thus are the seeds of Roman Calvinist guilt sown.

If you had pocket money (which I rarely did) you could give some of it to sponsor a black baby; give it a name, send money for school books, get letters of thanks, the full deal. Loads of girls in my class did. Their adopted babies probably ended up as presidents and politicians but they didn't keep in touch. Black or white, weans are all the same: they never write, they never phone, they never text, they never email, they never send you a message on Twitter.

It turned out my father was talking from experience on the subject of being hungry. His father had been killed in the Great War, which was what the First World War was called until the Second World War turned up. His mother, my Big Granny, did not take the loss of her husband too kindly and would occasionally resort to the drink.

Perhaps my Big Granny might have taken to the drink anyway, but the result was that there were spells when she was on the whisky and my father had to fend for himself. He knew what it was like to go hungry.

This was in the Gorbals in the 1920s and there was no shortage of pubs to which granny could send for a few gills of whisky. My father did not speak much about those days but when he did, it was with bitterness about people who would 'run the cutter'; people who would take money that should have been spent on food, to fetch more drink for his mother.

It wasn't all *Angela's Ashes* in their single-end in Errol Street. Maggie, my Big Granny was a hard-working hawker, which meant she went round the houses of wealthier Glasgow residents buying up their second-hand clothes.

Granny was at the top of her trade. She didn't just knock on doors. She was hawker by appointment to many well-off households. It was an arduous trade, carrying great bundles from the well-heeled suburbs back to the Gorbals, especially when an officious conductor would not allow her on the tram with her hawker's bundle.

Her haul was then classified into: quality items that would go on sale in the better second-hand shops; the middling stuff which went to Paddy's Market; and the rubbish which went to the rag store. My granny was a recycling heroine.

Being the second youngest of seven, I only really knew the Big Granny towards the end of her life. She was a gruff but kindly old lady who smelt of snuff and peppermints. The journey from House-hillwood, in the countryside, into the exotic, teeming streets of the Gorbals was like stepping into another world.

In her bijou studio flat, as they were not called in those days, Granny cooked on a coal-fire range. She would serve bowls of Irish stew from a blackened pot that never seemed to be empty.

She would send me and my brothers to the sweetie shop to spend the pennies we had been given for bus fares. Granny would pay on the return journey.

Then there were the times she smelt more of whisky than snuff and peppermints. One day, after telling me and brother Archie to blow our money for our fares on sweets, she reneged on the deal. She got on the bus without us and we had to walk five miles home.

When Granny had taken drink, you didn't want to be on the

receiving end of her catering. She was once left in charge of making us lunch. 'There are bananas and tomatoes. Just make them some sandwiches,' my mother said.

We came home and sampled, with some trepidation, granny's culinary creation — the banana and tomato piece; both ingredients mashed together between two slices of bread, with salt and pepper liberally applied.

With a wee dram in her, Granny would often sing a song the lyrics of which were: 'Who told you to fire that gun, Sergeant major number one . . .'

I did not get the poignance of this ditty at the time. I knew my grandfather had been killed in the war. I did not know he had been blown to bits.

John Shields had been a regular soldier and when the Great War was declared open by the eager combatant nations he re-enlisted in the Royal Horse Artillery and Royal Field Artillery. He left his wife and five-year-old son and his job in the Glasgow shipyards to go and fight for king and country. He was among the first to arrive on the battlefields, on 19 August 1914.

He was not mentioned in despatches. We know about his war mainly through the medals he was awarded. We are not talking about a V.C. or Military Medal like on the front page of the *Victor* comic. Gunner Shields, J., number 37575, got his medals for being there and for being killed.

When he died, he was serving in the 83rd Battery, part of the Lahore division of the Indian Corps. A Gorbals man in an Indian unit, which had been attached to the Canadian army. My grand-father died to preserve the empire.

To be precise, my grandfather perished in a fight over a small part of Belgium, a piece of elevated ground near a village called Zillebeke. The high bit was called Hill 60 on the military maps. The maps also had locations with names such as Glasgow Cross and Gourock Road, which must have made the Scottish soldiers feel at home.

Zillebeke today is a suburb of Ypres, a name with much reso-nance. Zillebeke is famous for being the place where so many German and British Empire soldiers died. One of the tourist land-marks is a massive bomb crater. There is also an amusement park with a rollercoaster.

The many citizens of Canada who gave their lives in and around Zillebeke are not forgotten. Near one of the memorials there is a restaurant called Canadian Pizza. The area is known for the hops from which the Belgians make their excellent beers. You might have a glass with your pizza.

Back in that lovely war, the hills around Zillebeke had been taken, lost and retaken on various occasions by both sides.

On 2 June 1916, the Germans initiated what became known as the Battle of Mount Sorrel. The 13th Wurttemberg Corps launched a carefully planned and stealthily prepared assault and overran the Canadian and British forces.

Wurttemberg is a region in south-west Germany. The capital is Stuttgart. I had my best ever time in Stuttgart following Celtic in the UEFA Cup. You could not have met nicer people. That was in 2004. In 1916, the Stuttgartians were busy trying to kill my grandfather before he had a chance to kill them.

A hand-written official account declares simply that on 2 June, his 83rd Lahore battery was 'badly knocked out' by the German artillery. They were hit by 900 shells on one day.

The diaries also report that the Canadians and British, and maybe some Indians, in the trenches fought to the last bullet in their handguns. They may have had little choice. An order had come they were not to retreat under any circumstances.

The order came from Brigadier-General Edward Spencer Hoare Nairne, the commanding officer. The brigadier-general survived the battle for Zillebeke. In fact, he lived to the ripe age of ninety and probably got to know his grandchildren. There is a painting of him in the National Portrait Gallery.

I am not bitter, really, about the different fates of Gunner Shields, J., number 37575 and Brigadier-General Edward Spencer Hoare Nairne.

It was the brigadier-general's job to be back at brigade HQ on 2 June 1916, telling his troops not to retreat. It was his luck to live to the age of ninety.

It was my gunner grandfather's job to be at the front line. It was his bad luck to die at the age of thirty-one.

Eric Bogle has a song where he is sitting by the graveside of Willie McBride, a nineteen-year-old soldier who was killed in 1916. Bogle's lyrics say: 'I hope you died quick and I hope you died clean. Or, Willie McBride, was it slow and obscene?' I love Mr Bogle's concerts when he comes back to his native Scotland from his adopted Australia, although it's very emotional when he does 'Willie McBride'. Sometimes it's good to have a wee greet.

A German soldier's eye-witness report of the early hours of the Battle of Mount Sorrel says: 'The whole enemy was a cloud of dust and dirt into which timber, tree trunks, weapons and equipment were continuously hurled up, and occasionally human bodies.'

It seems likely my grandfather died quickly but maybe not cleanly. They found no body. He has no known grave. He does have a plaque on the wall of the Menin Gate memorial at Ypres. Apparently Gunner Shields J., number 37575, is still due a medal he failed to collect.

Frankly, the British Empire can stick that medal right up their Menin Gate. I feel the same about the poppies which are touted on Remembrance Day in the name of Douglas Haig, the British commander-in-chief who presided over the slaughter.

Haig, apparently, was upset about the loss of life at the battle of Mount Sorrel. It got in the way of his plans for a much bigger event a month later on — the Somme.

One of my Big Granny's favourite tipples was Haig's whisky. She probably did not see the irony in her contributing to the profits of the booze company belonging to the family of the man who had callously sent her husband and so many soldiers to their deaths.

I never, ever bought a poppy from the Earl Haig Fund on the grounds that I had already donated a grandfather. The whisky company had a slogan: 'Don't be vague, choose Haig'. I preferred Liverpool poet Roger McGough's reworking of this: 'Don't be vague, blame General Haig.'

Gunner Shields J., number 37575, was just another piece of cannon fodder, unless you lived at 3 Errol Street in the Gorbals.

My father didn't remember much about his father. He was five when his old man went to war. He did remember, for the rest of his life, his mother's screams of despair when the telegram was delivered. And he remembered the years of hardship as she worked at her stall in Paddy's Market to make a living as a war widow.

My granny Maggie did get a scroll in honour of her husband from a grateful King George V. It extolled the bravery of those who 'left all that was dear to them, endured hardness, faced danger, and finally passed out of the sight of men by the path of duty and self-sacrifice, giving up their own lives that others might live in freedom'.

My father Charlie's legacy was a consuming passion for peace. He pursued this mainly through a life-long commitment to the Labour Party.

9

Father's toast and father's mince

One of the mysteries of my childhood diet was the paucity of fish and the almost complete absence of chicken. My mother was a fishmonger to trade. Even with all the children to tend, she found time to work part-time at various fish shops on the south side of Glasgow.

Like the cobbler's bairns being ill-shod, Annie the fish filleter's weans saw a bit of haddock or whiting on the occasional Friday but that was the extent of it.

The reason was that my mother spent long hours gutting fish and did not want to bring this work home. She had a particular dislike at her work of pulling the entrails out of chickens and other birds on sale at the shop. In our house, the chicken was an extinct species.

Her fish-filleting was conducted in the freezing cold. Her hands would be red raw with handling fish packed in ice. Her feet would be numb with the cold off the stone floors.

Just to make her life a bit more uncomfortable, one of her employers managed to spill neat, highly concentrated cleaning chemicals on the shop floor and burn the soles of her feet. She was a martyr to her feet thereafter. She could only get relief if her feet were gently massaged. Mercifully for her, with seven children and twenty-four grandchildren there was no shortage of volunteers for the ritual of rubbing nana's feet.

When there were only three of the seven weans left in the house, my mother was able to rest those feet a bit more. I think of those times as 'the *Ivanhoe* years'.

Annie developed a great fondness for the children's serials on STV. It was a throwback to happy times watching the matinees in the cinema in the Gorbals. *The Lone Ranger, The Cisco Kid, Champion the Wonder Horse* took her back to the wild west.

There was *Robin Hood,* the hero of Merrie England, and a young Roger Moore as *Ivanhoe,* the knight from days of old.

We had a street rhyme which went: 'In days of old when knights were bold/ And paper was not invented/ They'd wipe their ass on a clump of grass/ And walk away contented.'

I don't think my mother knew that one.

The *Ivanhoe* years brought a big difference to mother's mince. There was no 'Eat the Breid' to come home and dip outsiders into the pot. The mince boiled away merrily while mother watched the television.

We would come home to the theme tune 'Ivanhoe! Ivanhoe! To

adventure, bold adventure we will go . . .' And the unmistakable aroma of burnt mince.

Mother was a conservative kind of cook and didn't move on much from the basic menu of mince and stovies until late in her life when an Asian family moved in next door and would bring her various spicy dishes to try. She took kindly to curries and even went with her new neighbours on a visit to the mosque.

Her brief foray into Italian cuisine was not successful. Brother Archie had to stay overnight and had left an oven-ready pizza for his supper with instructions that it only needed heating up.

He returned to find mother had cooked the pizza in her traditional way. She had taken it out the plastic wrapping and put it in a pan of boiling water with an Oxo cube.

Fruit was a bit of a rarity for the working classes of Brock Road. It was often purchased when visitors were expected, to show you weren't poor really. The fruit would be kept in a bowl in the display cabinet.

A display cabinet was, as it sounds, a piece of furniture used to house any *objets d'art* or valuables a family may have. One lady from Govan, visiting her son who had got wealthy and moved to Pollokshields, went into his local butcher to buy a ham hough.

The butcher said that it would come in at seven shillings and sixpence, which was an awful lot of money. 'Naw thanks, it's for making soup, no' fur ma display cabinet,' she said.

The most likely way for a Househillwood urchin to get the required five a day fruit and veg was to wait until after dark and then quietly pillage any neighbourhood gardens that had apples, plums, gooseberries (commonly known as 'goosegogs'), brambles or any other purloinable items.

Another method, which was legal and occasionally affordable, was to buy chipped fruit from Galbraith's stores. Bruised and bashed apples, pears and sometimes bananas would have the dodgy bits cut off and the remnants sold at knockdown prices to a grateful peasantry.

The same deal was available from the bakery department where a large bag of broken biscuits could be had cheaply. These slightly damaged baked goods had seen service in the pick'n'mix biscuit department and were now being retired 'hurt'.

The first task was to search through the bag for any hint of chocolate but this was usually a rarity. There might be iced biscuits, or custard creams. There were usually some of those dark brown bourbons with the white filling.

Mostly it was plain digestive but no one was complaining because in those days a packet of full-price, unbroken biscuits was a rare treat.

There was a time when we had too many biscuits. It was when my father worked at the McDonald's factory making Penguins. Not the cute Antarctic creatures, the even cuter biscuit which not only had a chocolate coating but a chocolate cream filling.

The advertising slogan was 'P-p-p-pick up a Penguin!' The factory workers were allowed to p-p-p-pick up large quantities of Penguins for a p-p-p-pittance. These were the Penguins that had emerged misshapen or in some way less than p-p-p-perfect from the production line.

Legend has it that some workers were not content with this arrangement. Women would smuggle out perfect Penguins down their knickers, before the biscuits had got to the wrapping stage.

Legend also has it that Margaret Thatcher indulged in this practice. When she was a little girl called Margaret Roberts in Grantham, she attended a birthday party at which there was a generous spread and young Margaret attempted to take home some chocolate biscuits down her drawers. Her deceit was uncovered when the chocolate melted and dripped on to her socks.

Once we became affluent, we had plenty of biscuits that were not broken or misshapen. By affluent, I mean that my brothers and sisters still at home were working and I was a student on a government grant which more than covered my living expenses.

We had Jacobs Club biscuits, as in the TV advert: 'If you like a lot of chocolate on your biscuit, join our club. . .' We had Jammie Dodgers, sometimes even Jaffa cakes.

We had so many biscuits, that mother had to buy a big tin to hold them. It was no ordinary tin, but a biscuit barrel. One night, mother said to brother Archie, using a bit of Scots vernacular: 'Bring ben the biscuit barrel.'

Archie returned with the container and said: 'Here he is. Here's Ben, the biscuit barrel.' Thenceforth, over a cup of tea while watching the telly, the cry would go up: 'Somebody go and get Ben.' Ben had become part of the family.

McVittie's Jaffa cakes are sponge biscuits with a syrupy orange filling, half-covered in dark chocolate. They are pretty much irresistible.

When I think of Donald Dewar, Scotland's first First Minister, it is not as the creator of the modern Scottish parliament. It is of Donald as the man who ate all the Jaffa cakes.

His staff would set up the coffee and biscuits for a scheduled meeting in Donald's office. On more than occasion, the biscuits had to be replenished before the meeting started because Donald had scoffed the lot.

'Let them eat cake' was an instruction rarely heard in the Shields household. Cakes were a luxury item to be admired in the City Bakeries window but only occasionally to be encountered hands-on.

Nevertheless, we were expert cake-spotters. We could discuss

knowledgeably the ingredients and flavours of the Eiffel tower, the
fly cemetery, the pineapple cake, the meringue, the fern cake and
the empire biscuit.

There is a piece of folklore in the Shields family regarding cakes.
The scene was the living room in Brock Road, Househillwood, in
1952. A trestle table was laid out with the Co-op's finest fancies
as part of a wedding feast. A neighbour alerted my parents after
she noticed through the window that someone had started the
feast early. A little hand could be seen reaching from under the
table and purloining various of the goodies.

I cannot tell a lie. It was I who ate the Eiffel tower. Why this
cake is so-called is something of a mystery. It is not so much a
tower as a small turret of sponge drenched in jam, liberally dusted
with coconut and topped with a glacé cherry.

It is similar to the Australian lamington cake which is square
and not tower shaped.

An erudite colleague insists the Eiffel tower is related to the
French delicacy, the madeleine and quoted Marcel Proust on the
subject. In his autobiographical novel À la recherche du temps perdu,
Proust describes how the taste of those cakes evoked a vivid memory
of his aunt, who used to feed him madeleines on Sunday mornings
before mass, dipping them in her own teacup before passing them
to her nephew.

The French madeleine is baked in a cockleshell-shaped tin but,
my erudite colleague explained, the British version is done in a
dariole mould and is none other than my beloved Eiffel tower.

I once skipped an entire week of mathematics lectures when I was a student at Strathclyde University to sit in the library reading *À la recherche du temps perdu*. It truly was *temps perdu*. I eventually dropped out of my course with only two subjects short of a degree.

But I did learn a bit about Proust. As George Lemaitre said in his seminal work, *Four French Novelists*:

> A great part — perhaps the greatest — of Proust's writing is intended to show the havoc wrought in and round us by Time; and he succeeded amazingly not only in suggesting to the reader, but in making him actually feel, the universal decay invincibly creeping over everything and everybody with a kind of epic and horrible power.

This book, you may have noticed, is a kind of *À la recherche de Tom Shields perdu*.

I went in search of the Eiffel, the cake not the tower. They are off the menu in the high street bakers, but I eventually found some in Grant's bakery in sunny Dennistoun. Patissier Jim Entricen makes the little fellows by hand. For some reason, they are topped not by a glacé cherry but a jelly tot. That's the east end of Glasgow for you. We will forgive Mr Entricen this aberration, especially since he also makes the most wonderfully fluffy, doorstop-size tattie scones.

Another cake I most likely stole when I was only four at the wedding feast of my big sister Anna was a fly cemetery. This is a square of flaky pastry packed with a compote of intensely sweet raisins.

Bigger boys would tell you they were not raisins but dead flies which had had their wings removed and made into cakes by evil bakers. We were not put off the consumption of fly cemeteries by this nickname.

Well up in my list of favourite cakes is the meringue, the large and crumbly confections of sugar and egg white which manage to be chewy while melting in the mouth. They are also stuffed with that fake cream which is so bad for you.

What I like best about the meringue is a joke by Scottish comedian Andy Cameron. A man goes into the City Bakeries and asks: 'Is that a doughnut or ah'm a wrang?' The assistant says: 'No you're right. It's a doughnut.'

Sadly for my diabetic condition, the bakers' shops in Barcelona offer the most mountainous and toothsome meringues. I buy one very occasionally and cannot resist asking: '*Es que está es una merengue o me equivoco?*' (Is that a meringue or am I wrong?) To which they should say: '*Si, es una merengue.*' But they tend just to look puzzled.

Mother did not bake very often. It was always a bit of a thrill to come home and find she had out the bag of Lofty Peak flour, and the tin of Royal baking powder. The label had a picture of a tin of Royal baking powder. And this tin also had a picture of a tin of Royal baking powder. To look at a tin of Royal baking powder was to stare into infinity.

When mother baked she did so on an industrial scale. Her apple pie was thrown together in a large oven tray without recourse to recipes.

The only measurement involved would be its dimensions, usually about three square feet; with lashings of hot, runny custard it kept the natives quiet for a whole day.

But her *tour de force* was the dumpling, as seen in *The Broons* comic strip in the *Sunday Post*. Again, the ingredients were chucked in from memory.

In a huge baking bowl were assembled large quantities of currants and sultanas, sugar and syrup, cinnamon, ginger and nutmeg, flour and suet, and probably a few other mystery ingredients.

It is called a 'clootie' dumpling because the mixture is then wrapped up in a cloth, or 'cloot' in old Scots, and boiled in a large pan. Mother stuck her mixture into a suitably adapted pillowcase (to prevent the dumpling having two peaked corners instead of being spherical). She then put it in the clothes boiler (there were no washing machines in those days) for what seemed like far too many hours as far as a dumpling-crazed wee boy was concerned.

The dumpling was then put in a hot oven or in front of the fire to dry and develop its hard skin; an essential element of a real dumpling.

The glorious fusion of fruit and spices and the unctuousness of the suet makes dumpling a pudding beyond compare. But, like mince, it has become a pejorative term. But, call me a dumpling if you like; sweet, spicy, a bit fruity, warm, curvaceous, exciting and loved by all.

Dumplings could also be generous. They were usually made for birthday parties and to add to the fun thrupenny bits were added during the mixing process, adding a treasure-hunt element to the already high level of bliss.

There were still silver thrupennies about, although they were gradually being taken out of circulation. If you got a silver thrupenny, some adult would make the idiotic suggestion that you keep the coin as a souvenir instead of rushing to the nearest sweetie shop.

There was no such problem with the then-modern 'wooden' thrupenny which wasn't made of wood but of a yellow-brown metal. When times were tough, it was a penny or even a ha'penny you might find in the dumpling.

The coins were wrapped in waxed paper to prevent inadvertent swallowing. If swallowed, the recovery of the coins could be long and unpleasant process.

When I say waxed paper that sounds quite posh. 'Thomas, fetch the waxed paper whilst I mix the ingredients for the cloth dumpling,' my mother never said. The waxed paper was bits of the wrapper from a loaf of bread.

The wrapper had many uses, the most obvious being wrapping

up your play piece. It was also used to give a shine to the chute at the playground. The wax made the surface slippy and the descent much more thrilling, and frankly dangerous at times.

When there were no cakes, we could have a piece on jam, but even this was on the menu for a limited period after the weekly visit to the Co-op.

We didn't go shopping in those days. We went for the messages. It wasn't a family outing. We weans went for the messages with a long list which hardly varied from week to week. Our dividend number with the Glasgow South Co-operative Society was 77498.

Our message list included two pots of jam; one strawberry and one apple and rhubarb. The strawberry jam was first to be devoured; then we turned our attention to the cheaper variety.

When the jam ran out, a piece on margarine sprinkled with sugar could be substituted. It had to be margarine because the limited supply of butter in the weekly budget had been used up.

And it was just any margarine. It wasn't Stork, the leading brand. It was Echo, a cheaper and more industrial variety.

What concerned me most about Echo margarine was not its inferior quality nor its association with an element of poverty. It was the fact that Echo was not only spread on bread but was also used as an ointment for scabby knees.

Better than any cake or biscuit was a slice of warm toast, even with Echo margarine. Toast with jam and butter? Words like 'sheer' and 'bloody' and 'luxury' spring to mind.

In a big family on a modest budget, toast was a reliable and always available snack. My school chum Brian Hastie had an inordinate appetite for toast.

We would go to my house for toast of an evening. Then we would go to his house for more. The Hasties were more numerous even than the Shields. Brian had declared at an early age that he preferred his bread toasted only on one side.

He admitted it didn't taste as good, but with loads of brothers and sisters eagerly awaiting the output of the toaster, he got his ration more quickly.

There were times when I preferred my toast slow-cooked. That was on the nights when all of the family would sit round the fire. You would sit as close to the hearth as you dared, or were allowed, holding a fork with a piece of bread to the flames. If you were wee, my father would put your bread on an especially long fork and do the honours for you.

The magic of it all was that we sat round the fire with the lights out. I would stare entranced at the glowing coals and the flickering flames. Sometimes father would tell a story, occasionally slightly scary, about ghosts. Mostly it was happy stuff about the olden days.

Warm fire, warm toast, warm memories. It was much later I discovered that the firelight sessions were a way of saving money. There were times when my parents were literally counting the pennies to be able to feed the gas and electricity meters, and buy bread to feed us.

Father's toast was fabulous. Father's mince was as challenging as mother's mince. After surviving lung cancer in 1960, father took to buying stuff from a health food shop.

He introduced dates, prunes, pinhead oatmeal and other items into the Shields diet, which was fine until he started to put oatmeal into the mince and prunes into almost everything.

We revolted. But brother Archie and I, as teenagers with a burgeoning interest in ale, gave unswerving support to father's new hobby of making his own beer out of a kit from the health food shop.

Father did insist, however, that we didn't drink it straight from the fermentation bucket.

10

My life as an athlete

I imagined this chapter might be the shortest in the book.

My adult life has been largely free of any strenuous activity. There were a few games of football and the occasional round of golf in my twenties and thirties.

Football gave me up when I got too breathless and unfit. I gave up golf because I was not going to achieve anything more than a mediocre level.

For nearly thirty years, the closest I got to a work-out was a walk to the pub. My daily dozen was not a routine of calisthenics. It was the minimum number of alcoholic drinks I would have in a day.

But, as I looked back across my life, I realised I was not always such a sluggard. As a boy, I pursued a busy sporting life with my street pals in 1950s Glasgow.

My earliest memory of athletic activity was our own mini-marathon. It involved running round the 'block'. The block was the rectangle of houses in Brock Road, my street in House-hillwood, Glasgow, which served as our running track.

Our sporting events were seasonal or, more likely, inspired by some event in the news. I was six years old at the time of this great run. British athletes had just broken the four-minute mile barrier.

We became, briefly, distance runners, all little Roger Bannisters and Chris Brashers. It was not a case of the loneliness of the long-distance runner; not with about twenty of us pounding our way round the block.

Running was a regular feature of my early life. Mostly, it was running away from people. I would run away for fun in a street game of tig or hide-and-seek ('5, 10, 15, 20, 25, 30 . . . Here I come ready or not!').

Sometimes it was running away, out of necessity, from the famous Glesca polis, who seemed to devote an inordinate amount of time to preventing children from playing games, especially football, in the streets.

It is not as if we were hazards to traffic or traffic was a hazard to us. In Brock Road in the 1950s, you might see one car in an hour. Two vehicles together was rush-hour.

The constabulary would turn up on push bikes or on black scooters and give chase. We would escape up closes and into back gardens. The police rarely seemed to catch anyone. Maybe they knew it was a pointless exercise and they were going through the motions to placate complaining neighbours and the sergeant back at the station.

There was running away of a more urgent and desperate nature during my teenage years. Gang culture was rife in 1960s Glasgow with the carrying of what are now known as offensive weapons.

I certainly found the possibility of being stabbed quite offensive.

I was careful to keep away from these deranged people. Their insanity was self-documented with such gang graffiti as 'Mad Mental Tongs Rule Ya Bass'. You could steer clear of places where the gang members congregated, but there was always the prospect of being a random victim.

My father, in his sixties, was on his way home one night from a meeting for one of his many good works within the community when he was confronted by a bunch of youths. It was looking dodgy. Then he heard one of them say: 'No, leave him, he's too old.' And my father was allowed to pass.

He had been spared injury, disfigurement, or perhaps worse by a moment of relative decency and respect for age on the part of a young thug.

Strangely enough, while the local gendarmerie had a strict policy against street football, they were rarely to be seen in locations where the knives were out.

I'm not saying I lived in *Fort Apache, the Bronx*, although it is reputed that a dead and skinned gorilla was found in the street of a neighbouring Glasgow *arrondissement*, famous for the edginess of its thoroughfares. The discovery prompted a passer-by to comment philosophically: 'Well, that's Govan for you.'

Gorillas and human beings alike had to be ever vigilant and fleet of foot to avoid these young men of violence; young men who kept the ancient sport of duelling alive.

In the manner of William Wallace's warriors in *Braveheart*, the gang members were tooled up with a wide variety of arms. They carried knives mostly, but also machetes, hatchets, axes and swords.

Police reports tell of sabres, short swords, bayonets, cutlasses and the odd scimitar, which found their way into the hands of these young *chevaliers*. The classic Scottish weapon, the two-handed claymore, was thankfully too large an implement to conceal about the person on a social night out at the dancing.

A doctor at Glasgow Royal Infirmary casualty department, which of a weekend evening often resembled a military field hospital, wrote a thesis on the types of stab wounds he routinely treated. The title of his thesis was based on the reply he received on asking a patient what kind of weapon his assailant had used. The thesis was headed: 'Just an Ordinary Sword'. Phrases such as

cut-and-thrust and double-edged sword were not always meta-
phors in those days.

As children, we played war games that were slightly less blood-
thirsty. Prompted by some film or other about days of old when
knights were bold, we would go into medieval mode.

We donned armour which was home-made out of the big
National Dried Milk tins with which families were supplied to
feed the bairns in the decade after the Second World War.

The tins were flattened and turned inside out and fashioned into
breast-plates and helmets that glinted in the sun, just like in *El
Cid*.

With a large wooden pole, liberated from a nearby garden fence,
pressed into service as a jousting lance and a dustbin lid as a shield,
we engaged in chivalric combat, just like Roger Moore in *Ivanhoe*
on the telly.

There was an element of danger in this jousting especially when
it was your turn to be the horse.

If you weren't Ivanhoe, you could be Robin Hood. Archery was
another part of the curriculum. We fashioned our longbows from
tall garden canes, sometimes purchased at the corner shop but
often purloined from a fruit or vegetable patch (along with the
fruit and veg). The canes were cut in half to make arrows.

Health and safety regulations were lax in those days, but parents
would insist that the arrows were rendered slightly less dangerous

by the addition of a rubber tip, traditionally fabricated from the seal of a ginger bottle.

Despite this safety feature, the DIY bow and arrow remained a potentially ferocious weapon. More than one small person fell to a one-in-the-eye war wound similar to that suffered by King Harold at the battle of Hastings. But, being Scottish, we didn't do Saxons versus Normans.

Our conflict of choice was cowboys versus injuns. On the Wild West front, the weapons did not have to be home-made. The cowboy outfit was a common Christmas or birthday gift. There was no shortage of Colt 45s and holsters, wee Stetson hats, neckerchiefs in the style of Tom Mix, and sheriff's badges. Maybe even a plastic Winchester rifle and a set of spurs, again making it hell to be the horse.

The Red Indians, as we called them before we knew they were Native Americans, made their own weaponry. The bow that used to belong to Robin Hood was now in the capable hands of one of Sitting Bull's braves at the Little Bighorn or maybe Chingachgook from *The Last of the Mohicans*. A perfectly serviceable injun tomahawk could be formed from a small part of wooden fence and a flattened Heinz beans tin.

Most of us preferred to be cowboys rather than injuns. But I am sure if we had known about Wounded Knee and all that ethnic cleansing, we would have less keen to be part of John Wayne's seventh cavalry.

In the 1950s, we seemed to spend a lot of time still fighting the Second World War. The war was still fresh in the memories of adults. For us children who missed it, there were constant reminders via films with Audie Murphy as a GI hero. Our weekly comics, such as *The Victor* were full of storylines about brave British Tommies killing German soldiers in hand-to-hand combat.

The Germans usually died with an oath upon their lips such as '*Gott in Himmel!*' or '*Donner und Blitzen!*' Sometimes a simple 'Arrrrrrrrrrgggggh!' would suffice. Japanese soldiers were wont to scream 'Aieeeee!' or 'Banzai!' There we were, still in primary school, but fluent in German and Japanese epithets.

In our Second World War battle re-enactments, the bit of fence that used to be a jousting lance became a rifle. A bigger bit of wood could be a bazooka. Any missile that could be lobbed with relative safety became a hand grenade to destroy the enemy machine-gun post.

I don't remember anybody ever playing the part of the Germans or Japanese. So we must have been units of the British or US army all shooting at each other. It was friendly fire and we didn't know it.

Whether we were cowboys or commandos, one of the more popular war games was the contest to see who could die in the most entertaining manner.

The ideal location for this game was a grassy slope. The contestants would run up and at the person who held the imaginary gun, and who was also adjudicator of the competition. The idea was to fall theatrically to the ground as if hit by a sniper. (This little game is still played to this day by professional footballers all over the world.)

On reflection, this dying game was a gruesome re-enactment of newsreel footage of First World War soldiers charging from a trench into a hail of bullets and shell. Or the carnage of the D-Day landings. Or Robert Capa's photograph of the Moment of Death in the Spanish Civil War.

But it was quite a compelling activity, especially if you won the Oscar for best death.

I started off writing about sport and exercise and wandered into the realms of childhood martial fantasy. But the bottom line of all these imagined wars was that they involved a lot of running about and a great deal of imagination. Much better than sitting at home fighting gory battles on your computer or play station.

We did fit in quite a lot sport in between our wars. We played golf. This was usually inspired by coverage of the Open Championship or those challenge matches on television with Arnold Palmer, Gary Player and Jack Nicklaus.

Ours was urban golf and not the game as played at the Royal &
Ancient. That bit of fence, which had already seen service as a jousting
lance and a rifle, now became a golf club. It was driver, mashie niblick
and putter all in one. The ball was of the tennis variety.

The golf course consisted of the streets and pavements of Brock
Road. The aim of the game was to propel the tennis ball along a
tarmacadam fairway up to a concrete green and into the hole,
which was in fact a drain cover, or 'stank' as we called it.

As well as this street crazy golf, we would occasionally get to
play on green ground with actual golf clubs and balls. There was
putting, and pitch and putt in many of Glasgow's fine public parks.
In our early teens, we graduated to the odd round of golf at one
of Glasgow's municipal courses, usually Deaconsbank.

The course was then a pretty scabby landscape of short grass,
long grass and no grass, much derided by members of private golf
clubs, but to us it was Royal Deaconsbank and as epic a challenge
as St Andrews or Troon was to proper golfers.

Our set of clubs (and it was often just the one set between a
foursome) more than matched the modest surroundings. In our
mangy bag there would be an ancient hickory driver, thread hanging
off and held together by insulation tape, and a mongrel collection
of irons, some bearing well-known brands such as Slazenger or
Wilson but many had the name Glasgow Parks stamped on them.
The balls we used were hand-me-downs and resembled misshapen
potatoes rather than the pristine spherical objects used by Arnold
Palmer and company.

A round at Royal Deaconsbank cost the outrageous amount of four shillings so the budget extended to only the occasional game. You could try to sneak on to the course but the park rangers who checked for valid tickets were ever vigilant and harsh on illegal urchin golfers.

A useful ploy was to lurk in the woods around the back end of the course and take advantage of a lull in fairway traffic to play a few holes. The fifteenth at Deaconsbank ran beside some woods and was particularly suitable. We emerged from the trees on to the tee, hit a lightning two-iron on to the green, raced down and used the two-iron to putt out before melting away again into the woods.

These guerrilla golf tactics came in handy much later in life for my only triumph in the sport when I beat a colleague, the *Glasgow Herald* golf correspondent and a serious player, in the annual office knock-out competition.

I had the choice of venue and this proper golfer, used to lush greenswards, was discomfited by the basic nature of Deaconsbank.

He was especially miffed when urchins stole his ball from the first fairway. I insisted he incur penalty strokes on the basis that if he didn't want his ball stolen by wee boys emerging from the undergrowth, he shouldn't hit the thing so far.

My dear colleague gave up the ghost when I hit a two-iron at the fifteenth, ran down to the green and putted with my two-iron for a birdie to go three up with three holes to play.

We played cricket in the long, hot summers even when it was long and hot and raining which could happen in Scotland even before global warming. We used tennis balls rather than cricket balls, which are hard and harmful objects when moving at speed. We weren't scared of cricket balls or anything; it's just we didn't have any.

Often we didn't have cricket bats either. And, you've probably guessed, yet another bit of wood from a fence would be used as a substitute. Whether it was a lump of wood or a proper cricket bat, there was always the danger of collateral damage.

Many a young wicket-keeper got too close to the action and got a bat in the mouth. The threat 'Do you want a bat in the mouth?' I believe passed into oral tradition (if you will pardon the pun) through our version of cricket.

We did not play the game according to any rules in the *Wisden Cricketers' Almanack*. If you smote the ball into the long grass and it got lost, you could notch up as many runs as you liked.

A Househillwood test match could last for ages, or could end unexpectedly when a batsman got tired of plodding up and down to score fifty runs off one ball, or if the fielders went home in the huff.

More popular than cricket was a game of rounders which is like baseball or soft ball. All you needed to play rounders was a simple bit of fence as a bat and a tennis ball. And, as the name suggests, you ran round a lot.

Rounders was more popular because the teams included girls as well as boys. A game of rounders could end in an unscheduled, but perhaps predictable, fashion when male and female participants would head off into the long grass in search of a lost ball and not come back out until hours later.

We did play tennis, usually when Wimbledon was going on. Yes, it was with tennis balls, and usually with real, if slightly beaten-up, tennis racquets. We didn't have a proper net. Instead,we used what was left of that garden fence.

We did mountaineering and rock climbing, without leaving our urban environment. The hills we climbed were actually large brick air raid shelters which were to be found in many back gardens; remnants of that war I seemed to have mentioned quite a lot in this chapter.

Other slopes we conquered were attached to bridges or aqueducts. One of the rites of passage involved ascending one of these slopes and then 'dreeping' to the ground from the highest point.

Look up dreeping on your Internet dictionary and it will tell it is a word concocted by James Joyce in *Ulysses*, a mixture of creeping and dripping. This was not our dreeping. We hadn't got round to reading Joyce. Look further and you will find a poem by Adam

McNaughtan called 'Where Is the Glasgow that I Once Knew?' Adam talks about 'dreeping aff a dyke.'

A dyke is a wall. Dreeping is the process of dangling from a height and letting go. Dreeping was usually done with eyes closed and in a state of some trepidation.

You dreeped, you took the plunge, because the fear of being ridiculed by your peers was worse than the thought of hurting yourself. It was a terrifying and at the same time exhilarating experience. It is only when you return as an adult to the scenes of your derring-do, that you realise it wasn't that high; not such a big dreep after all.

We did Formula 1. Our vehicles were called 'bogies'. Or 'cairties', if you were Oor Wullie (Fat Boab in my case) from the *Sunday Post* cartoon strip.

A bogie was a sports car made out of a plank of wood attached to two sets of pram wheels by flattened-out tin cans. Steering was done by a length of clothes rope tied on to the front axle. Braking was done by applying the soles of your shoes to the front wheels.

There were no safety helmets or kneepads. When your bogie overturned at speed, which was a regular occurrence, it was skinned knees all round and maybe a few milk teeth left scattered on the pavement.

The horsepower to propel the bogie came from your pals who

pushed ferociously from behind. This was the element of aerobic exercise which made our version of Formula 1 such a healthy, if scary, pursuit.

We had bikes, of course. Few of us ever got a new shop-bought cycle, so we made our own with cannibalised parts.

The construction was done with the help of a big brother or a neighbour who worked in an engineering factory or shipyard — when Scotland was still one of the workshops of the world — and who had the practical expertise and the tools. It was recycling in every sense of the word.

Of necessity, some of these machines were very basic. My first bike was built on a handsome maroon Hudson frame with the requisite number of wheels, a seat and a set of straight handlebars. It looked as cool as any modern mountain bike costing hundreds of pounds.

What my bike did not have was a set of rear brakes, which are kind of essential for coming to a steady and safe stop. One day, engaged in a race round the block (which for the occasion had ceased to be an athletics track and was now a velodrome) I was going far too fast to take a corner. I pulled on my front brakes far too suddenly and discovered that Newtonian law of physics about how every action has a reaction which is equal and opposite.

I discovered that if you are going at speed on a bike and you yank hard on the front brakes, the bike stops but you continue over the handlebars in a forward motion. It was a case of more skinned knees but no serious injury since I was lucky enough to have my fall broken by a garden hedge.

Looking back, I cannot work out how we managed to fit in so many eclectic sporting pursuits. For I also remember that we played football all day, every day.

The matches could be epic encounters down at the public park, with jerseys for goal-posts. Teams could be twenty-five a side or more, since no one who turned up was denied a game.

The duration of the game was flexible. You could play for a couple of hours, go home, have your tea and come back to find the match still in progress.

The final whistle (metaphorical since there were no referees and no whistles) came when it got too dark to play on. You might then go on for a warm-down kick about under the street lights which would last until parents came out to conduct a final round-up of children they probably had not seen (apart from essential fuel stops) since early that morning.

As well as the full-blown matches involving multitudes, there were continual tournaments of 'heidies' (games of headed football conducted in more confined spaces). These were usually only one or two persons on each side and were relatively brief with nineteen goals half-time, thirty-nine the winner being a popular designation of length.

As a footballer, I was keen but not very good. I managed to get selected for my school football team but as a full-back, a position which more accomplished exponents were not interested in filling. The only thing worse than being a right back was being left back, holding the jackets.

I was just glad to be in the team and not at all jealous of those to whom God had given greater skills. I was proud of Alex McColl, our dazzling right-winger who in his early teens had attracted the attention of scouts from Arsenal football club.

I was in awe of the natural football brain of Joe McDermott, a scheming midfielder before the term scheming midfielder had been invented. Unfortunately, other parts of Joe's brain did not work quite so effectively and he would forget to get out of bed in time for the Saturday morning matches in the schools' league.

It was the days before substitutions were allowed. Mr Harry McKeown, our team coach at St Robert's primary, would start the game with ten men hoping that the delinquent McDermott would eventually turn up.

Mr Joe McLean, our coach at Bellarmine secondary, did the same. Or he would delay kick-off as long as possible while a messenger was dispatched to rouse the sleepy McDermott from his bed.

Both my football managers, Messrs McKeown and McLean, were incredibly supportive of my attempts. In a team debriefing after a particularly lacklustre performance, Mr McLean lambasted his talented players for lack of effort. He said they should follow my example when it came to effort. 'Shields never stopped trying,' Mr McLean said in what was my greatest footballing moment. 'He didn't make contact with the ball at any point but he never let the opposing left-winger get by him.' I think the referee noticed this as well. But they didn't give out many red cards to wee boys in those days.

My career in top-flight schools football was short and insalubrious. I only scored one goal and that was against my own team in the first round of the Scottish Schools Cup. It was what I thought to be a cleverly crafted header back to my goalkeeper. But the goalie was only about four feet high and the ball sailed into the net.

Our gym teacher, a Mr Harry Morgan, who wasn't even the team coach, took it upon himself to berate me in public for my lack of talent. It was at that point I realized that P.E. teachers were not recruited for their brains or subtlety.

I got my revenge on Mr Morgan by refusing to make any effort in his class, pointedly knocking over rather than jumping over the hurdles on the athletics track. He got his revenge by giving me six of the belt 'for dumb insolence'.

I got my revenge by saying, 'You would know about dumb insolence, sir' as he meted out the punishment. And so it went on until, many years later, I realised that Mr Morgan wasn't really a bad guy, just an enthusiast who should have been in the SAS regiment rather than a teacher.

It was at the time of my public humiliation after the own-goal incident that I decided to improve my footballing skills. By assiduous practice, I could emulate my hero Pat Crerand, a classy midfielder then gracing the green-and-white hoops of Celtic, who went on to win a European Cup medal with Manchester United.

I had read that a good way to develop passing skills was to spend hours aiming the ball at a designated object such as a dustbin.

Eventually, I became reasonably proficient at striking the ball towards dustbins with a reasonable rate of accuracy. I dropped out of being a right back in the school first team in favour of being a midfield player in the ragbag assortment that made up the second team.

I was still totally out of my depth but deliriously happy about playing at right-half, just like Crerand. If only we had played against a team of dustbins, we might have won the occasional game.

As well as the football, golf, tennis, Formula 1, cycling, cricket, rounders, archery, jousting, mountaineering, war games and long-distance running, we found time for our very favourite pastime of 'hinging aboot'. This, I suppose, was our equivalent of hanging out down at the mall.

We did indeed hang about at shopping centres, or just shops in the street as they were known in those days. We would hone our shoplifting skills at Woolworths, the chain store of fond memory.

But mostly we would hing aboot on green ground, parks, gardens and farmland. We would chase and catch butterflies and keep them in jam jars where they would quickly die. We hunted hedges and collected caterpillars which we put in jam jars and watched them turn into butterflies and quickly die. We seldom thought to set them free.

We collected bumble bees and kept them in jam jars and got stung for our acquisitive cruelties. We caught wee fish from the Brock Burn, minnows and bigger catfish, and put them in jam jars, where they died. Looking back, I think wee boys with jam jars were an ecological disaster on a par with global warming.

The point I am making here, at some length, is that we got plenty of exercise. I may have been a bit fat but I was fit. When I became an adult, I put aside these childish things. I got fatter and less fit because I forgot to go out and play.

11

Trust me, I'm an astrologer

Gout was the first adult disease I was stricken down with. Gout is the painful condition where uric acid in the blood crystallises to form little daggers on the sufferer's joints, principally the big toe. The little daggers stab away ferociously; the surrounding area becomes inflamed. It is certainly the most pain I have ever been in. Sydney Smith, a chronicler of the condition, said the pain was like walking on his eyeballs.

However, gout is a source of humour for cartoonists. The subject of the fun is usually some crusty old aristocrat who has been over-doing the crusty old port and is now confined to a bath chair with a foot swaddled in bandages. It was known as the rich man's disease or the patrician malady.

It was quite appropriate, therefore, that my gout was diagnosed when I was at the Badminton Horse Trials. I was at this event to observe the landed gentry and the rich at play. Sadly, they do not play badminton on horseback which might be diverting. The sport involves them falling off horses while trying to negotiate sheer fences and impossibly dangerous obstacles at breakneck (sometimes literally) speed.

But I was the casualty with a very sore big toe. I went to the medical tent where I was seen by a veterinary surgeon. He diagnosed gout, a subject in which he was expert although he usually only treated horses. He gave me some painkillers, human not horse-sized. He advised me to get some loose footwear.

So I ended up hobbling around the horsey event in a pair of green wellingtons. Sadly, not the fashionable, leg-hugging variety with buckles, as favoured by Sloane Rangers. I had to go for big, loose, green wellies without any buckles.

In these wellies, I look more like Mellors the gardener than Lord Chatterley. Actually, I am not sure if there is a lordly husband in *Lady Chatterley's Lover*. I only read the shagging bits.

There is an amusing greetings card which is quite rude but nevertheless suitable to send to any woman who has, or has had, a gardener. The Mellors character is standing to attention (in more ways than one) with his trousers at his ankles. He asks: 'Will there be anything else, m'lady?'

I was in pain but relieved it was gout and not arthritis. After all, as Lord Chesterfield (the man who invented the sofa) said: 'Gout is the distemper of a gentleman, whereas rheumatism is the distemper of a hackney coachman.'

Those who know my disinterest in watching any sport other than football may wonder why I was at the Badminton Horse Trials. I was on the run from the World Snooker Championship in Sheffield. I had gone to the snooker finals at the Crucible in Sheffield hoping to find fascinating Runyonesque figures to write about.

But all I could find were snooker anoraks, corporate sponsors and players who were too smart to get involved in Runyonesque behaviour, which might compromise their chances of a big pay day.

I did briefly find some diversion in Sheffield when I went to see Arthur Scargill, president of the National Union of Mineworkers, move into his new offices in the city. Scargill was a bit of a working-class hero in those days. There was no one quite like Arthur for appearing on *Any Questions* or *Newsnight* to tweak the noses of the capitalists.

Shortly after being elected president of the miners' union, Arthur moved the union headquarters from London to Sheffield. I abandoned the snooker to watch the removal men carry Scargill's goods and chattels into his new abode.

Arthur was very chatty to the reporters who had gathered to record the event, but he was more interested in the TV cameras. There were quite a few takes as Arthur was filmed carrying a portrait of himself. He was not a shy man.

Scargill ceased to be a hero during the miners' strike of 1984 when he sent his members to the slaughter against Margaret Thatcher's Tory government. Scargill's generalship of that campaign showed all the callousness, lack of subtlety and blind egotism of a First World War military strategist.

CHRONIC GOUT.—To Cure.—"Take hot vinegar, and put into it all the table salt which it will dissolve, and bathe the parts affected with a soft piece of flannel. Rub in with the hand, and dry the foot, etc., by the fire. Repeat this operation four times in the 24 hours, 15 minutes each time, for four days; then twice a day for the same period; then once, and follow this rule whenever the symptoms show themselves at any future time."

The philosophy of the above formula is as follows: Chronic gout proceeds from the obstruction of the free circulation of the blood (in the parts affected) by the deposit of a chalky substance, which is generally understood to be a carbonate and phosphate of lime. Vinegar and salt dissolve these; and the old chronic compound is broken up. The carbonate of lime, etc., become acetate and muriate, and these being soluble, are taken up by the circulating system, and discharged by secretion. This fact will be seen by the gouty joints becoming less in bulk until they assume their natural size. During this process, the stomach and bowels should be occasionally regulated by a gentle purgative. Abstinence from spiritous libations; exercise in the open air, and especially in the morning; freely bathing the whole surface; eating only the plainest food, and occupying the time by study, or useful employment, are very desirable assistants.

Meanwhile, the Badminton Horse Trials painkillers had worked a treat. The gout had gone so I forgot about it. I didn't to go the doctor. I didn't even take the trouble to read up on the condition.

The gout came back quickly to punish me. It was on a visit to Turin on the occasion of the Italian city's twinning with Glasgow. Twinning was big business in those days. Glasgow's Lord Provost was forever having to drag himself and his entourage off to Rostov-on-Don in Russia, Dalian in China, Nuremberg in Germany, or wherever, for municipal sibling celebrations.

As a journalist, I was suitably condemnatory of the waste of ratepayers' money that these trips involved. Luckily, my trip to Italy was funded by the ratepayers of Turin (if people pay rates in Turin), so my conscience was clear and my journalistic ethics unsullied.

My condition and my big toe flared up to such an extent that I had to borrow a walking stick from a doyen travel journalist who was in his late seventies but was getting about Turin in a much more sprightly fashion than I was.

My gout meant I missed a visit to the opera in Turin. There were not enough tickets to go round so I volunteered to stand down on medical grounds. I did, however, ignore my disability and dragged myself to the alternative to the opera which was a trip to the Stadio delle Alpi to watch Juventus — with Michel Platini, Zibigniew Boniek and Claudio Gentile in the team — play Udinese in a Serie A game.

Platini and Boniek were fine exponents of attacking football, but as a full-back to trade myself, I only had eyes for the defender Gentile. Claudio was a most accomplished player and is said to be the best man-marker ever. In a career of marking opponents, often indelibly, he never received a red card.

The score was 4–1 to Juve. My delight at the match was increased to no end by a vendor with a large vacuum flask attached to his back who came round dispensing wee cups of hot black coffee and brandy. I had quite a few medicinal *coretti*.

Un coretto is the Italian for an espresso coffee with a shot of alcohol. The Spanish word is *carajillo*. In Scottish coffee shops, it is called 'Ye Cannae Huv Wan. We're No Licenced.'

I left Turin in a wheelchair, full of brandy to kill the pain but still full of pain.

> **11.** **Soot Coffee**—Has cured many cases of Ague, after "every-thing else" had failed. It is made as follows:
>
> Soot scraped from a chimney, (that from stove-pipes does not do,) 1 tablespoon, steeped in water 1 pt., and settled with 1 egg beaten up in a little water, as for other coffee, with sugar and cream, 3 times daily with the meals, in place of other coffee.
>
> It has come in very much to aid restoration in Typhoid Fever, bad cases of Jaundice, Dyspepsia, etc., etc.
>
> Many persons will stick up their noses at these "old grandmother prescriptions," but I tell many "upstart physicians" that our grand-mothers are carrying more information out of the world, by their deaths, than will ever be possessed by this class of "sniffers," and *I* really thank God, so do *thousands* of others, that He has enabled *me*, in this work, to reclaim such an amount of it for the benefit of the world.

Gout is an idiopathic illness. From the Greek word *idios*, it means arising spontaneously. In my case, it was idiopathic as in 'idiot'. My method of coping with gout way back then was to drink quite a lot of lager to kill the pain.

I was saved from this path of idiocy by an astrologer. Darlinda, or Rita Madhok to use her off-duty name, was an immensely popular columnist in the *Sunday Mail* informing readers about how your Venus was rising and if the moon was in Uranus.

Darlinda also had a flourishing private clientele who came along for readings. Rita took her astrology seriously, but did not take herself too seriously.

Rita suffered from ill-health, particularly kidney failure. She spent much of her spare time raising funds for research at the renal clinic at Glasgow Western Infirmary. Rita died in 1995, but the work of the charity goes on and £700,000 has been raised.

Rita had seen me hobbling into the Caprese restaurant in Glasgow and came over to ask me what was wrong with my leg. I explained it was gout and she immediately referred me to a consultant.

The consultant was her husband Rajan Madhok who just happened to be one of the top men in the field of rheumatism, arthritis and gout. Dr Madhok, or Raj as he preferred to be known, got me off my idiopathic self-treatment with alcohol and on to a proper treatment regime.

The long-term process of dealing with gout is simple and pain-less. You take one tablet, such as Allopurinol, each day. This medicine decreases the amount of uric acid in the blood and, with luck, acute attacks of gout will be few and far between.

In the olden days, before it was known that drugs could control uric acid levels people suffered mightily from the sharp crystals which formed on the joints.

These painful shards were called *tophi*, which is Latin for stones. The chalky nodules could grow so big that they stuck out from under the skin. In Victorian times, it was not unusual for a foot-baller to be unfit to play because of gout. In such cases, the sports pages would report that the individual 'cannot play for tophi'. This is the origin of the modern usage of someone who 'can't play for toffee'.

I made up that last bit about tophi. But most of the stuff in this book is generally accurate, or as accurate as you are going to get from someone who has worked as a journalist for forty years.

What is for sure is that via one illness or another I have ended up with elbows that look like Mr Punch's chin. Some people say they look strange and I should cover them up and not wear short-sleeve shirts, but I think they look quite distinguished; a bit like the elbow version of a prominent Roman nose. One medical source attributes my odd-shaped elbows to tophi. Another says it is bursitis, which is an inflammation of the wee sac which works the hinge at my elbow.

Either way, it has not unduly impaired my elbow-raising activities over the years.

This one little pill has thus taken away a lot of the mystique and much of the legend which had built up around gout over the centuries.

The onset of gout was once put down to 'excessive venery', which is olde-English for too much shagging. This is, of course, a load of old bollocks.

More liberal attitudes prevail these days. A Sheffield NHS trust has launched an initiative aimed at schoolchildren, emphasising the health benefits which can accrue from sexual activity.

Their leaflet, entitled *Pleasure*, declares: 'An orgasm a day keeps the doctor away.' It contains the advice: 'Health promotion experts advocate five portions of fruit and veg a day and thirty minutes' physical activity three times a week. What about sex or mastur-bation twice a week?' This is something of a change from Victorian warnings that DIY sex was the cause of blindness, madness, impo-tence and hairy hands.

SPERMATORRHŒA.—A discharge of seminal fluid, commonly called seminal weakness or debility. It is only of late years that the true nature of this disease has been properly understood, many of the most serious cases having been regarded as and treated for *gonorrhœa*, which, though indeed the proper name of the disease, is a term now confined to an unhealthy discharge from the lining membrane of the *urethra*, a discharge which, when long standing and chronic, becomes a gleet, and is *always the result of infection*. Spermatorrhœa, on the contrary, proceeds from an injury inflicted on the organs of reproduction, and consists of a discharge from the spermatic and seminal vessels, and may be entirely, and in many cases is, completely irrespective of all venereal taint.

Spermatorrhœa is a disease that could hardly, by any possibility, arise in a natural way; no organic affection of the part, no amount of debility, or complication of accident or disease, indeed, could produce what is called seminal emissions, did not the patient, by incontinence or vice, provoke the cause, and engender the disease himself. Many men are so inordinate in their passions, that in time they amount to a mental disease, such as we have already characterized under the name of *satyriasis*, an intemperance which, if given way to, so debilitates their bodies and paralyses the seminal organs, that whether unduly excited or in a state of temporary rest, they are kept in a condition of constant irritation and involuntary excitation; thus, whether sleeping or waking, often from the most trivial contact, indeed from the mere force of the imagination alone, those debilitating emissions, which constitute the most important feature of this disease, are repeatedly taking place. But though incontinence in youth is often the cause of spermatorrhœa, the disorganization of the spermatic system, and the ruin of connubial happiness, it is unfortunately to the vice of self-pollution, that moral offense known as onanism, that we must in general attribute that moral prostration and physical incapacity now so wide spread among the youth of the present generation, and of which the disease we are at present considering is only one of the lamentable evidences.

We had intended to devote a space of this work to the injury inflicted on the reproductive organs by the inconsiderate folly of youth, but for reasons which will be readily understood by all who remember the strictly domestic nature of this work, we have deemed it best to embody the pith of what we might have said on such a subject in this place, as being more pertinent to the theme, and at the same time keeping the pages of the Recipe Book generally free from what, to

It would now seem that excessive venery might be a useful tool in the prevention of gout.

The traditional perception is that gout is caused by eating too much rich food and drinking too much alcohol. I would certainly have fitted this profile.

One of the most famous gout-sufferers was Henry VIII, who in his lifetime changed from being a sylph-like handsome prince to a fat and unhealthy old man. I made much the same journey, from relatively sylph-like handsome student to fat old man.

In a photograph taken when I was made an honorary doctor of

> **2. Laudanum.**—Best Turkey opium, 1 oz.; slice, and pour upon it boiling water, 1 gill, and work it in a bowl or mortar until it is dissolved; then pour it into the bottle, and with alcohol of seventy-six per cent. proof, ½ pt., rinse the dish, adding the alcohol to the preparation, shaking well, and in twenty-four hours it will be ready for use. Dose.—From 10 to 30 drops for adults, according to the strength of patient, or severity of the pain.
>
> Thirty drops of this laudanum will be equal to one grain of opium. And this is a much better way to prepare it than putting the opium into alcohol, or any other spirits alone, for in that case much of the opium does not dissolve. See the remarks occurring after "Godfrey's Cordial."

Strathclyde University, I was wearing the graduation gear of a gown and hood and silly hat and I looked a dead ringer for the old Henry VIII.

Obesity and excessive consumption of alcohol are still listed as factors in developing gout, but it is not down to corporeal excess alone. Robert Walpole, Britain's first prime minister, was an example of how gout 'can be got by the thin and temperate'.

In the olden days, publications on how to deal with gout were as popular as diet books and DVDs are today. One solid piece of advice for a gout-free life was: 'Live on sixpence a day — and earn it.'

I prefer the pamphlet called *Laugh and Lye Down; or a Pleasant but sure Remedy for the Gout without Expence or Danger*. It was written by William Brownsword in 1739. If he was alive today, Mr Brownsword might be writing this book instead of me.

Gout can run in the family. Archie McArthur, my maternal grandfather, was a sufferer. My affliction may be hereditary. Except that no one else in a large family has it.

Maybe I just inherited his lifestyle. Archie, or my Wee Grandpa

as he was known, was from Skye. Like many a Skyeman, he liked a drink. He worked as a drayman at a distillery in Port Dundas in Glasgow so was never shot of the opportunity to have a wee dram or, more likely, a very large dram.

The Wee Grandpa was doubly unlucky with his gout. One winter morning he was leading his dray, laden with whisky barrels from the distillery, down the icy streets to the ships waiting at the docks. His Clydesdale horse lost its footing and fell on top of the Wee Grandpa. One of poor Archie's legs was crushed and had to be amputated. It was the good leg, the one in which he never got the gout attacks.

The gout sufferer will always be prone to sudden acute attacks. Pain-killers usually bring relief but sometimes the remedy is an injection straight into the knee, or big toe, or other affected joint.

I don't want to go into too much information here, but for an acute attack my preferred analgesic (anal being the operative word) is the suppository.

Suppositories can be painful. It certainly was for me the night of an acute attack as I was rolling about on a hotel bed trying to administer the bullet when I fell out and cracked my head on the marble floor.

This was in Perugia where I went to watch Dundee FC play in a European football tie. Turin, Perugia, the Caprese restaurant. I'm beginning to think Italy and the Italians are to blame for my gout.

12

Snoring for Scotland

Snoring is no joke, although those who are blissfully free from the complaint seem to think it is. I speak as one who suffers mightily. When I doze off on an aeroplane, anxious passengers summon a steward to ask why the engines are making such a terrible noise.

I once fell asleep at a football match (not difficult since it was Partick Thistle against Forfar) and made more racket than the rest of the crowd (again not too difficult on a dour winter's afternoon at Firhill).

Then there is the embarrassment factor. Snoring loudly through the guitar solo at the children's school concert. Making an unscheduled contribution to the soundtrack at the cinema, usually during a quiet and poignant moment. Waking up with a loud snort in a railway carriage to the general amusement of your fellow passengers. Worrying if my snoring is keeping people off their work at the factory across the road.

There is also the inconvenience, when I was an office-bound

person, of not being able to retreat to my cubby-hole for a wee sleep after lunch. The noise would have been something of a give-away.

When you are a mega-snorer there is also the fact that you try to stay awake until others are asleep. Many's the time I have had to stay up for hours in the bar of an overnight train or ferry out of consideration for others.

In a hotel at Calais in the wee hours of the morning, I was wakened by a banging at the door. It was the irate occupant of the next room. In the course of a short but animated conversation I learnt the word *ronfleur*, for snorer. And some other phrases which appeared to be a request to put an effen sock in it.

I love the potential for conflict which arises from the average Scot's lack of knowledge of foreign languages. A young footballer

whose team had just won the final of a schools' tournament in France suddenly lashed out at an opponent as the two sides shook hands after the match.

The young Scot explained in mitigation to his team coach: 'Sir, he swore at me.' The French player, in his turn, said he had merely been congratulating his adversary on being a *vainqueur*.

It wasn't just that my snoring sounded like a lumberjack using a chain saw. I was emitting loud grunts and gasps for breath. That's what an eye (or ear) witness told me. I was asleep and unaware of the ructions.

The embarrassment was compounded by the fact that I snored because I was fat and drank too much. At least that is what a kindly acquaintance told me. He knew because he had read about it on the Internet.

When I did my own research, I discovered I was not merely an Olympic class snorer. I suffered from sleep apnoea.

Sleep apnoea is when you stop breathing through the night. During an apnoea, the muscles in the throat relax and cause a total blockage of the throat's airway. An apnoea usually lasts for around ten seconds. The brain is starved of oxygen and sends an emergency wake-up jolt to the body. No wonder I had so many dreams that I was dying.

A sufferer can have as many as ten apnoeas an hour. You are not refreshed for the next day. My sleep apnoea could have killed me. I fell asleep at the wheel while driving from Aberdeen to Glasgow.

Thankfully, it was not when I was doing 70mph. I was wakened by a comparatively gentle bump into the car in front as I drew up at traffic lights on the outskirts of the city.

The incident persuaded me finally to get my disturbed nights seen to. There was help at hand at the Glasgow Royal Infirmary sleep disorder clinic. After an examination which was a wee lie-in while connected to various devices, I was declared apnoeaic, or whatever the term is.

The clinic equipped me with a continuous positive airway pressure (CPAP) machine. This bit of kit blows air through a tube into a face mask. The benefit is that you do get a good night's sleep.

The problem is that you go to bed looking, as Her Indoors said, 'like the Creature from the Blue Lagoon'. She meant *The Creature from the Black Lagoon*, the horror film. The Blue Lagoon is a chip shop in Glasgow.

The CPAP mask with its long dangling hosepipe has the advantage that it can be used to frighten children. But many kids think it's a hoot. Notably Seorcha, Joe and Cal who, when I stayed in their house in Montpellier, would ask: 'Go on, Tom, do your elephant man.'

The sleep equipment is not just a mask attached to a wind machine. To stop the throat becoming too dry, the air has to be passed through a humidifier. To stop the humid air from being too cold, the water chamber has to sit on a wee electric heater.

Then you have to get an insulating sleeve on the connecting hose to prevent condensation which causes 'rainout' or drops of water shooting up your nose. Uncomfortable, but better than thinking you're dying in your sleep.

The entire device can look like something out of Dr Franken-stein's workshop. When you're travelling you have to take the whole kit and caboodle with you, taking up valuable luggage space that could be used for transporting bottles of rioja and brandy. But the CPAP machine does work and some days I'm so refreshed I have difficulty getting over for my afternoon nap.

A lucrative snoring industry has developed. There are many offers of miracle cures. These can come in the form of gum shields or 'mandibular advancement devices', which sounds better when you are paying £50 for a lump of plastic. Or nasal strips, bits of stain-less steel you stick up your nostrils, throat and nasal sprays,

and even a simple rubber chin strap to keep your trap shut.

The sellers of such products give cheerful warnings that snoring can lead to brain damage, heart attacks and strokes. At the very least you will suffer from headaches, memory loss, chronic fatigue, personality changes and relationship stress.

The miracle cures tend to have ingenious names which are based on the word snore and contain quite a few Zs. The devices come with enthusiastic endorsements about how lives have been changed and marriages saved.

A quick search through users' forums will show that disappointment and no refund is often the result of purchase. If it's too good to be true, it usually isn't true.

There are surgical solutions for snoring. I studied the merits of uvulopalatopharyngoplasty versus sequential uvulopalatoplasty. Then there is the non-surgical injection snoreplasty.

This uvulopalatopharyngoplasty is quite drastic. The surgeon cuts out your tonsils, soft tissue at the back of the throat and the uvula. I'm not really sure what the uvula is but I'd rather keep mine the way God gave it to me.

Possible side effects of this uvulopalatopharyngoplasty are pain, bleeding and risk of infection, not to mention drainage of secretions into the nose. Your voice may develop a nasal quality.

Patients who have had the uvula removed will become unable to speak French correctly or any other language that has a uvular

> **Cold—To Avoid Catching.**—Accustom yourself to the use of sponging with cold water every morning on first getting out of bed, followed with a good deal of rubbing with a wet towel. It has considerable effect in giving tone to the skin, and maintaining a proper action in it, and proves a safeguard to the injurious influence of cold and sudden change of temperature. Sir Astley Cooper said, "The methods by which I have preserved my own health are—temperance, early rising, and sponging the body every morning with cold water, immediately after getting out of bed; a practice which I have adopted for thirty years without ever catching cold."

'r' phoneme. To which the answer is *merde*, I think I'll stick to being the man in the mask.

One cure which works but is not recommended:

An oil rig worker suffered from a terrible sore throat whenever he was working offshore. He awoke each morning with a nasty taste in his mouth. He had an irritating cough which lasted all day long.

Naturally he was worried about this, and each time he went on leave he would get himself along to the doctor. But the doctor could never find anything wrong.

The chap was beginning to fear the worst. Back on the rig, the sore throat came back. He confided his fears to his workmates as they sat at their tea.

At this point the workmate with whom he shared a room said that it was time he came clean. The sore throats were probably his fault. He explained: 'I can't get to sleep for your loud snoring. So, one night when you were lying on your back, mouth open, I dropped some soap powder down your throat. It stopped the noise so I've been using it ever since.'

Thin people snore too but it is generally recognised that obesity is a major factor. Over-consumption of alcohol can exacerbate the condition.

If you don't want to snore, don't get fat and don't get drunk.

13

The private memoirs and confessions of an unjustified drinker

This story of a man who went the whole Hogg (hope you haven't missed the literary allusion here) begins in June 1964 when I was sixteen years old and decided to go to a pub for the first time.

The excuse was to celebrate the end of the O Grade examinations. The pub crawl started in the Atholl Arms, which was one of Glasgow's many temples to alcohol; all carved wood, smoke and mirrors.

The main concern was not to appear under-age. It helped that my partner in crime (whom I will not name since he is now a teacher in a posh school) was a big lad with a voice so husky you would have thought he smoked forty Senior Service a day.

A problem was the bewildering selection of drinks available. There was light beer which was a dark colour, and heavy beer which looked a lot lighter than the light beer. There was wee heavy, which turned out to be the strongest beer of all.

One Scottish beer is called eighty shilling. This term is a reference to the amount of liquor tax which used to be levied according to the strength of the alcohol. In the days of the old money, the shorthand version of eighty shillings was 80/-.

This format is still used to describe the beer on pub dispensing taps and on price lists. It can be confusing for young people who are decimalised and know nothing of shillings. Like the latter-day lad trying to buy an under-age drink, who was refused when he ordered a 'pint of eight zero forward slash hyphen'.

On that first venture to the pub, we were going to have a beer of some sort and steer well clear of the whisky, which most of the men in bunnets in the Atholl were consuming in great quantities. Harp lager was being widely advertised back in those days as a drink for bright young things. My pal asked the barman for two Harps, which the barman obviously misheard as 'two halfs' and served us quarter-gills of whisky.

The stuff was a severe challenge to the teenage palate. It must have been hard-going for the seasoned adults as well because there were free bottles of lemonade on the bar to dilute and sweeten the spirit and make it drinkable.

So much for the mystique of Scotch and the nuances of our national drink. Most of the customers were drinking whisky as an alcopop.

Our next port of call was Sloan's bar in Argyle Street which, we had been told, served the best Guinness in town. Sloan's had magnificent booths where schoolboy drinkers could hide their naivety, which was just as well because the pints of dark and bitter-tasting stout were also too much of a challenge.

If the barman had seen us diluting the black stuff with lashings of lemonade, we would likely have been out on our ears. Real drinkers don't do Guinness shandies.

Alcohol is an acquired taste. I managed to acquire the taste through practice and perseverance. I like a drink. I must do otherwise I would not have spent such a large proportion of my adult life in pubs.

The average kidnap victim is separated from their family for a shorter spell than some of my sojourns in licensed premises. Let's not go into how much money I spent. Suffice to say that if my loved ones had paid the publicans a ransom, it would have been less than my bar bill.

My personal best for the amount of time spent in the pub is eight hours and thirty minutes out of a reporting shift lasting eight hours and forty-five minutes. It would have been eight hours and forty minutes but the bar closed.

So that day my routine was: check in at office at 4 p.m.; put jacket over the back of my chair; go down to the pub at 4.05 p.m.; drink until ejected from at 12.35 a.m.; check back in at the office for ten minutes. I think we then went to the casino for a drink after work.

If my employers at the *Glasgow Herald* had tried to make

> **DELIRIUM TREMENS.—To Obtain Sleep.—**Give an emetic of ipecacuanha, then give 15 to 18 grs. of the same, every 2 hours, using the shower bath, and giving all the beef tea the patient desires.
> The jail Physician of Chicago reports thirty-six favorable cases treated as above. In Boston, at the "House of Correction," the danger arising from the sudden loss of their accustomed stimulus, according to Puritanic economy, is overcome by administering, freely, a strong decoction of wormwood.
> **2. Stimulating Anodyne.—**Sulphate of quinine, 12 grs.; sulphate of morphine, 1 gr.; mix, and divide into 6 powders. DOSE.—One powder every hour.
> Prof. King, of Cincinnati, O., says that from two to four powders of the above anodyne, will nearly every time produce sleep in this whisky delirium.

journalists stay in the office for eight and a half hours at a time, the union would have had us out on strike quoting the Factories Act, the Abolition of Slavery Bill and the European Declaration of Human Rights.

Those were the days before Mrs Thatcher's Tory government not so much moved the goalposts on trade union power but removed them entirely. Those were the days when the National Union of Journalists had power and would use it to secure an ever shorter working week, longer holidays and the maximum possible extraction of money from the newspaper owners' pockets.

The NUJ also protected individual rights. One of the times we stopped the paper was because a reporter had been sacked for persistently being drunk on duty.

On reflection, the management had a good case. The chap involved would spend even longer than I did in the pub. He would return to finish his late shift with a half-bottle of whisky. He would sit at his desk singing 'Who's Been Polishing the Sun?' as he polished off his carry-out. Then he would phone a taxi to take him home.

The NUJ, thankfully, had a zero tolerance policy towards members being sacked. It was an approach based on the Pastor Martin Niemoller theory of resistance to Hitler's regime: 'First they came for the drunk in the corner singing "Who's Been Polishing the Sun?" and I did nothing . . .'

Print journalism is different these days. The NUJ has little power but is still fighting a rearguard action to protect livelihoods in a declining industry.

The unions are wary of hitting the cobbles — an archaic expression for going on strike — even to save jobs. The prospect of industrial action to protect a drunken individual is unthinkable.

So, it is just as well that journalists have changed too. Most of the younger breed would rather spend hours in the gym than in the pub, but they do look forward to a drink. You will hear them say: 'I could murder a mineral water.'

My main tipple in a drinking career spanning forty-five years was lager. The amount of lager I used to drink was murdering me. On a long shift in the pub, I could shift ten pints. That is two and a half gallons of liquid.

Evil regimes are accused of torture under the Geneva Convention for forcing prisoners to ingest so much liquid. It's called water-boarding.

Ten pints of lager-boarding is equivalent to 2,000 calories. Add a couple of packets of crisps and you have reached the recommended daily calorific intake for a man.

Traditional Scottish drinking lore has it that real men don't do lumpy stuff and eating is cheating, but I liked to eat as well as drink. So those 2,000 lager-sourced calories were a bonus. Since my only exercise was walking to and from the pub, I didn't burn off the calories and I got fat.

My daily dose of lager on a working day could be as low as five pints. I was a bit of an amateur compared to one colleague who could sink twenty-five pints as he fitted work in between visits to the pub.

I was an amateur because I only had the one jacket. Professional topers had two; one to wear when ducking out of the office and one to leave over the back of the chair. People would say: 'He must be around somewhere. There's his jacket.'

I had an office avoidance technique of my own. I would arise betimes and put on an excessively bright shirt in the Hawaiian style. I would go into the office and make a point of going round talking to colleagues in many different departments. I could then disappear but workmates would say: 'Yes, Shields was in earlier. He'll be around somewhere.'

I learned this philosophy from my late friend Harry McLevy, a legendary Dundee shipyard worker and latterly engineering union official. Harry said: 'If you get a reputation for being at your work early you can spend the rest of the day in bed.'

George Best, the footballer with the huge talent, good looks and champagne lifestyle, made possibly the best comment on the drinker's lifestyle. When asked what happened to the cash he had earned, Best replied: 'I spent a lot of money on booze, birds and fast cars. The rest I just squandered.'

A large number of the people who travel to watch the Scotland football team have chosen to portray themselves in a military fashion. The main characteristic of the Tartan Army is that they drink a lot. Whilst on manoeuvres (as they say) at the world cup in Spain in 1982, a local person, intrigued by the amount of alcohol being consumed, asked: 'How much does beer cost in Scotland?' The Tartan Army person replied: "About £150 a week." At that time the exchange rate in Scotland was about £1.50 to the pint.

I was not a major player when it came to spending money in the pub. I didn't qualify for the 'free' Christmas lunch in the pub near the *Glasgow Herald*. To qualify for the 'free' lunch, you had to be in the £10,000-a-year bracket of expenditure over the bar.

However much money I frittered away on booze, my children always had shoes. They also had a dog, a Labrador called Libby, who used to eat their shoes. They got more shoes and eventually the dog discovered there were more interesting snacks than Clark's sandals.

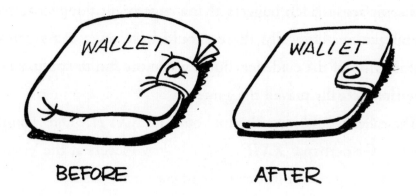

BEFORE   AFTER

There was always food on the table. The dog would eat that as well given half a chance. My food was often in the dog or in the bin when the pub proved too much of an attraction.

What concerns me more, on reflection, was not the waste of money but the waste of time. My excuse for spending so much time on manoeuvres was that I was in search of material for a humorous column.

I must have had many interesting conversations over all those hours and pints of lager. They certainly must have seemed fascinating at the time.

All those unforgettable times in the pub. I wish I could remember them.

I remember a bloke told me the body generates enough electricity to run a TV set. He couldn't tell me exactly how to connect body to TV set, but I imagine it involves attaching a pair of jumpleads to the nipples. I am still not sure where the earth wire goes.

There was a debate, I recall, about the assertion by a fellow drinker that the ancient Romans played bingo. I don't ask how this topic arose. Such nuggets of information just appear in pub confabulation. Logically, there should have ensued a rigorous examination of the evidence. But it was more fun to speculate on how they actually played the game.

The caller would have shouted out: '*LXXXVIII. Dues famines amplest.*' Or perhaps, '*XXII. Two little dux.*' Players at the Voguus Maximus bingo amphitheatre would cry out: '*Domus!*'

It would have been a time-consuming business doing the bingo in Roman numerals, not to mention cumbersome, since the bingo card would be in the form of a very large wax tablet. The main thing would be always to let emperors such as Nero or Caligula win. They wouldn't like losing. There is no point in scooping the jackpot with all those *librae, solidi* and *denarii* if you end up at the Coliseum being fed to the lions.

This same bloke often spoke Latin after a few pints. He said that some twenty centuries ago Tacitus had predicted financial problems for Rangers Football Club.

Tacitus wrote (something like): '*Sed Rangii, vagos et incuriosos, in clade intumbunt.*' Which means: 'But the Rangers tribe, wreckless and feckless, fell into a disaster.'

Here are some other topics I have heard discussed before my very ears, mostly in the Doublet Bar in Park Road, Glasgow:

Carrots used to be white until Dutch botanists did a bit of bio-engineering and made them orange in honour of King Billy.

Hiawatha was really crabbit. Not for nothing was he known as The Beast of the Woods.

King Arthur, the round table fellow, lived in Govan for part of his life. Merlin, his druidic adviser, came from Drumchapel, which made communication difficult since there was no direct bus link.

The arse will finally fall out of the Antarctic climate change-wise in June 2020, probably on a Tuesday which, with the ensuing flooding, means the Doublet quiz will have to be held upstairs in the lounge.

I must have laughed a lot over those pints of lager. I remember Bob Callander telling me about the man who was not happy at his wife spending a large amount of money on a bust-enhancing cream. 'Why don't you just rub some toilet paper between your breasts?' he said. 'Will that make my bust bigger?' she asked. 'It has certainly worked for your arse,' the husband replied.

Laura Stewart told me the true story of the boy who used to play truant and would while away the hours over a can of Coke in her Glasgow tearoom. Laura did not want to turn the wee fellow in to the authorities but equally she didn't like to see him missing out on learning.

She got him some books, including an atlas in which he became particularly engrossed. While he pored over the maps, Laura engaged him in some geographical conversation. The boy was talking about the Middle East. 'Where is Egypt?' she asked. 'It's on page 33, the boy said.

Like the boy in the tearoom, I think I was playing truant hiding in the pub all those hours of all those years.

14

Dis-thingmy-a

There is a story, widely disseminated on the Internet, about a man called Alistair McGregor who was being treated for depression in a New York hospital. McGregor had been diagnosed as suffering from Pervasive Negative Anticipation, a belief that everything will turn out for the worst.

Doctors tried to treat him with medication and counselling but with no success. The last option was electro-convulsive therapy.

Just as they were about to plug McGregor into the mains, a nurse, who was a fan of comedian Chic Murray, intervened. The nurse said: 'I don't think this patient is depressed, he's just Scottish.'

Chic Murray was from Greenock which probably gave him a head start on his career as being a wonderfully surreal, morose and funny entertainer. Chic's conservation was never mundane. Asked how he was keeping, he would say: 'Fine, apart from a wee touch of diarrhoea.'

When I had a wee bout of that pervasive negative anticipation, I told people: 'I'm fine apart from a wee touch of depression.'

The story about the Scotsman who wasn't depressed is most likely apocryphal. There is another widely circulated version with the exact same details about a Finnish patient in California.

In the Finnish version, there is no mention of a comedian. Perhaps Finland does not have a Chic Murray, which is very sad.

I like Finland and the Finnish. Wherever you go in the world and whatever bar you go into, you meet a drunk and maudlin Scotsman. Usually, at the other end of the bar there is a Finn who is more drunk and more maudlin.

I met a Finn in Malaga one January. He was living very comfortably off the money he got sent each month from the Helsinki unemployment exchange. He was supposed to be looking for work but spent all day on the beach and all night drinking vodka.

I told him he looked very happy for a Finnish person. 'So I should be,' he said. 'Back home my fellow unemployed are up to their arses in snow and can't afford too much vodka.'

I was lucky I didn't have major depressive disorder, which is a chronic and long-lasting illness. I just got fed up.

My self-diagnosis is that I caught my depression from my work. The job I did at the *Glasgow Herald* involved writing wee stories that were supposed to be humorous.

In search of these wee stories, I had to go to lunch with people and turn up at book launches, wine tastings, charity dinners, film premieres, theatrical opening nights, anywhere where there was a glass of wine, a canapé and crack of the verbal variety.

It all sounds rather jolly but in truth it is no fun trying to be funny all the time. My sanity was saved by having benevolent bosses who recognised that occasionally the comedian wants to play *Hamlet*. I was allowed to drop the wee jokes and write a rant about, for instance, the Evita-fication of Princess Diana by the British media in the days after her death.

On particularly dark news days, such as the school shootings in Dunblane or when the Pan Am jet fell on Lockerbie, a wise and understanding boss knows it is not a time for wee stories. The purveyors of jokes for the Diary are relieved of their duties.

Unfortunately for me, there was no wise and benevolent boss around on the day the airplanes crashed into the Twin Towers in New York. I was ordered to write a funny column because those

DELIRIUM TREMENS.—This is the disease of drunkards, and those who take narcotics, as opium, etc. It may be called "the *brain fever of drunkards*." The person is tremulous, has nausea, vomiting and wakefulness, restlessness; he raves, and imagines snakes, demons, etc., are about him. This disease doubtless arises from extreme stimulus of the brain.

To Cure.—First allay the paroxysm, calm and support the nervous system, by giving brandy and other spirits. The redness of the face, and the pulsation of the arteries, heart, etc., indicate determination of blood to the head. Equalize the circulation by bathing the feet and legs in warm lye-water; then apply mustard plasters to the feet and nape of the neck. Give a purge; and now and then a cup of valerian, scullcap, or strong hop tea, or from 10 to 20 drops of laudanum. Emetics are very useful, and may be given in the same kind of spirits the patient has been accustomed to take. A strong decoction of wormwood is successfully used in hospitals.

in charge had decreed that they wanted the rest of the newspaper 'to be as normal as possible'.

It was a patently ludicrous instruction, but I eventually did as I was told and have regretted it ever since.

The events of 9/11 changed my life forever, as it did for so many people, not because I was involved, but because I was ordered not to get involved.

My career as Tom Shields, gatherer of *bons mots* for the *Herald Diary*, ended that day. The depression which had probably been waiting in the wings took over.

There were little, tell-tale signs, like bursting into tears for no apparent reason at a dinner. I took to hibernating in bed, even though it was a nice sunny afternoon out there.

Some of my reluctance to get out of bed was due to an excessive consumption of alcohol the night before. But the main motivation was to avoid going into an office where the journalists were no longer in charge of the asylum. The accountants were in charge. Fun was not on the budget.

What was doubly depressing was that my employers were stuffing the pockets of various colleagues with large amounts of money to get them out the door and off the payroll. My request for similar treatment was denied.

Lying in bed all day can be a depressing and worrying business. I could do quite a lot of work by telephone and laptop, but I knew I would have to show face at some point.

Being in bed all day naturally involves a lot of dozing off while you're listening to Radio 4. The really scary bit is when I woke up in a darkened room to the theme tune from *The Archers*. Was it the 2 p.m. edition and time I was getting into the office? Or was it the 7 p.m. show and I had a slight problem meeting my deadline?

So I went to see my doctor and felt better almost immediately. It is amazing how beneficial it is to have a doctor's line that says you're too crazy to go to your work.

A medical man, not my own GP but a Lanarkshire chap who is the Rhodes scholar of the sick note, advised me not to return to work too soon. 'Very often, it is the second thirteen-week line that gets the result,' he said, referring to my efforts to get a redundancy deal.

But, cursed as I am with a Roman Calvinist work ethic, I went back to the job to work my notice. I had decided to leave the *Glasgow Herald* after thirty years.

I left without the large lump of money but with the chance to work part-time for the *Sunday Herald*. There were many advantages in this move. The *Sunday Herald*, by definition, only came out once a week. The editor, Andrew Jaspan, was very much in charge of the asylum and, crucially, believed that journalism was fun.

One of the hardest things about my little clouds of depression was discovering who were not really my friends: the people who did

not keep in touch; the people who kept away because they feared the condition might be contagious.

We should look after each other more. Tom Leonard, the writer and philosopher, says so in one of his *Six Glasgow Poems*.

It is titled 'Cold, Isn't It?' and goes:

> *wirraw init thigithir missyz*
> *geezyir kross*

My GP is a wonderful man who remains cheerful through all my illnesses. He doesn't seem to mind when I quote great chunks of Dr Google at him, although he does kind of prefer that at the end of the consultation I take his word for things rather than some website.

All the doctor could do for my little black clouds was prescribe some anti-depressants. He is apparently not allowed to say 'For God's sake pull yourself together.' Apparently that's only permitted when a patient comes in and says: 'Doctor, I keep thinking I'm a pair of curtains.'

I got some good advice from a friend who stood by me, usually in the pub. He advised me to stop taking the tablets. The anti-depressants were making me act more than a bit vacant and seemed to be making me more depressed.

I chucked the pills in the bin. Chucked alcohol yet again. And I started going for long walks to disperse the clouds. On these walks I kept meeting people who insisted on telling me how well I was looking.

With all the walking and much less alcohol consumption I lost weight.

In my new working regime, I didn't have to go into an office. For the first time in twenty-five years I didn't have to listen when people said to me: 'I've got a great story for your Diary column.'

My new editor thought it was a really good idea that I should go and spend weeks at a time working from my flat in Barcelona. Unaccountably, I got a lot cheerier. I was back to being merely morose.

I read up on depression. I realized how lucky I was that I had been able to make changes before my state of mental health deteriorated further.

I read how depression can strike even the most successful and focused people. Like Graeme Obree, the world champion cyclist, who I had envisaged as a buccaneering type of individual making his super bikes out of washing-machine parts.

He was the Flying Scot, full of drive and self-assurance who took on the establishment and won the gold medal, but privately he was riven with depression and had made three attempts at suicide.

I read that even apparently high-flying people suffer from a lack of self-esteem.

I had that lack of self-esteem in spades. People seemed to like the stuff I had been writing in the *Glasgow Herald*. They even bought lots of books containing material that had already been in the newspaper, but I felt my work was worthless.

I saw a giant poster one day in a bookshop advertising 'The new Tom Shields'. I should have been chuffed but I felt a deep panic.

This was not just a case of making sure you don't believe your own publicity. Or remembering that fame (even low level and localised as in my case) was okay as long as you didn't inhale. I never felt I was any good.

Thousands of books and millions of words have been written about how to change negative thoughts about yourself to positive ones. I read a few of these and discarded all of the advice.

I have developed my own technique. Whenever I feel myself falling into a spiral of self-criticism, I look at myself in the mirror.

I call on my deep reserves of Scottishness and I say: 'Well, Tam, you're no the worst.'

My research leads me to conclude that what I have is dysthymia. This is a chronic mood disorder that falls within the depression syndrome.

Dysthymia is a type of low-grade depression. I probably chose a low-grade condition because of my low self-esteem. Dysthymia is a Greek word for 'bad state of mind' or 'ill humour'.

I have renamed the condition Dys-thingmy-a after the good Scots word 'thingmy'. Thingmy is a general word applied to persons, items, locations, abstract nouns, concrete nouns, transitive verbs, intransitive verbs, concepts and precepts when people cannot remember who, what, or where they are talking about. I call my condition Dys-thingmy-a because I am not certain what I am talking about.

The main point about the use of thingmy is that the speaker assumes knowledge on the part of the listener.

An example might be: 'Thingmy took the thingmy doon tae the thingmy tae get it thingmied but it was thingmied.' This means somebody took something somewhere to get something done to it but it was not possible for some reason.

When asked to elucidate, the speaker will say, exasperated by the listener's slow-wittedness: 'Who? You know, Thingmy.' Or 'What? That thingmy.' Or 'Where? Doon the thingmy.'

I love to hear New Scots, as we call people from other countries and cultures who have come to live here, use old Scots words. As I walked along Garnethill Street, I saw and heard a Muslim woman pause from scrubbing her doorstep and shout over her shoulder: 'Rashid, bring me the thingmy.'

Scottish Muslim women are fantastic. I have met so many who are feisty, beautiful, just a wee bit domineering and passionate about all sorts of issues.

I may not have dys-thingmy-a. It may just be something called Learned Helplessness. This is when depression results from a perceived lack of control over events.

It is when people have learned to behave helplessly, even when the opportunity is restored for them to help themselves by avoiding an unpleasant or harmful circumstance to which they have been subjected.

I was mostly helpless through drink. Or as Dr Wikipedia puts it:

Learned helplessness can effectively contribute to poor health when people neglect diet, exercise and medical treatment, falsely believing they have no power to change. The more people perceive events as uncontrollable and unpredictable, the more stress they experience, and the less hope they feel about making changes in their life.

People with a pessimistic explanatory style tend to be poor at problem-solving. And as for cognitive restructuring? Please don't go there.

I got depressed when I read how Seligman and Maier, two psychologists at Pennsylvania University, tested their theory of learned helplessness.

Three groups of dogs were placed in harnesses. Group One dogs were simply put in the harnesses for a period of time and later released. Groups Two and Three consisted of 'yoked pairs'.

A dog in Group Two would be intentionally subjected to pain by being given electric shocks, which the dog could end by pressing a lever.

A Group Three dog was wired in parallel with a Group Two dog, receiving shocks of identical intensity and duration, but his lever didn't stop the electric shocks. To a dog in Group Three, it seemed that the shock ended at random, because it was his paired dog in Group Two that was causing it to stop. For Group Three dogs, the shock was apparently 'inescapable.'

Group One and Group Two dogs quickly recovered from the experience, but Group Three dogs, who could not stop the shocks, learned to be helpless and exhibited symptoms similar to chronic clinical depression.

I think I might get depressed if I were a dog whose life had consisted of wondering where the next Bonio was coming from and suddenly you are slightly more preoccupied by why you are being subjected to random excruciating electric shocks.

I am very fond of dogs but don't have one because you have to go round after them picking up their shit. That surreal comic Chic Murray solved this problem by having an invisible dog. When he met people in the street while walking his invisible dog, he would ask them to hold the invisible lead. When they did, he would say: 'Fooled them again, Rover.'

Another Chic Murray canine routine was: 'I went to this hotel. The sign outside said "Dogs must be carried". I thought where the hell am I going to find a dog at this time of night?'

Chic tells how he was stopped in London by a passer-by and asked: 'Do you know the Battersea dog's home?' Chic replied: 'I didn't know it had been away.'

Winston Churchill suffered from deep depression which he called his 'black dog'. The great British wartime leader dealt with his condition though compulsive overwork and excessive drinking. Maybe he should have taken the black dog for a long walk.

15

Flaky science

Dandruff has been part of my life for many years. It is a condition thankfully mitigated by Head & Shoulders. But, especially in later years as the skin dries and disintegrates, there will always be gentle drifts of dead skin on the upper slopes of the shoulders.

These integumental snowflakes are even more noticeable on those of us who prefer to wear black T-shirts. I used to worry about the social disadvantages and thought of buying clothes in shades of dandruff, then I could say that dandruff was the new black. Now, apart from clearing away the more egregious lumps of desiccated flesh, I have learned to live with it. Plus it gives my dear and caring niece Anne-Marie, who is a schoolteacher, something to do at family gatherings, flicking the detritus off Uncle Tom's shoulders.

There is good news for those who suffer from dandruff — scientists have finally cracked the genetic code of the fungus that causes

> **Baldness.**—The cause of baldness is defect in the hair follicles, from which the hair is developed. Sometimes it is the result of disease, and is frequently hereditary. Those who perspire much about the head are generally bald. If the hair falls off after fever, shaving a few times will tend to promote the growth. Keeping the head closely wrapped prevents the growth of hair. A drachm of the tincture of cantharides mixed with an ounce of lard, is a good application. An infusion of the *Asarum Europeum* Asarabacca, may be used as a lotion for the scalp.
>
> Rub the bald part frequently with the juice of an onion till it looks red; or, water, 1 pt.; pearlash, half an ounce; onion juice, 1 gill; rum, half a gill; oil of rosemary, 20 drops. Rub the head hard with a rough linen towel dipped in the mixture; or, take 4 ozs. of castor oil, 8 ozs. best rum, 30 drops oil of lavender, apply occasionally to the head, shaking the bottle well; or, beef marrow, well washed, melted, and strained, ¼ lb.; tincture of cantharides, 1 oz.; oil of bergamot, 12 drops. Wash the head frequently with warm water and Windsor soap; or with a decoction of rosemary and southern-wood.
>
> **Baldness.**—Rub the part morning and evening with onions, till it is red, and afterwards with honey; or, wash it with a decoction of boxwood; or, electrify it daily.
>
> **Baldness.**—Infuse for a few days, 1 dr. of powdered cantharides in 1 oz. of proof spirit; beef marrow, ½ lb.; soak in several waters, lastly in weak salt and water; melt, strain, and mix, adding 10 or 12 drops of oil of bergamot, or lavender.

the flakes. With the genome of the said fungus species, *Malassezia globosa*, now identified, scientists can proceed to a cure.

These scientists, it should be said, work for Procter & Gamble, who make shampoo and may have a vested interest in this issue.

From what I can ascertain, dandruff is a perfectly natural bodily by-product.

There are about ten million of these *Malassezia globosa* fungi on the average napper. The fungi eat stuff called sebum, which is an oily substance produced by the sebaceous glands of the skin. Sebum is made of fat and the debris of dead cells and sounds as if it could be part of the Scottish diet.

The fungi excrete oleic acid, which as you know is a mono-unsaturated omega-9 fatty acid. The oleic acid causes a larger than normal amount of skin cells to be made, causing more dead cells than normal to be produced, which is the recipe for dandruff.

The scientists also discovered that the fungi have the genetic ability to mate.

So, consider what may be going on in your flowing locks: the *Malassezia globosa* are not only dining well on your sebum, they are also indulging in a spot of houghmagandie.

It wouldn't surprise me if the scientists discovered the fungi were also having a wee sherry before dinner and a post-coital cigarette. They may be having conversations along the lines of: 'How was it for me, darling? The earth moved so much I nearly fell off on to that bloke's shoulder.' It could be that our dandruff is having a better time than we are.

16

It's a funny thing, drink

Alcohol can add to the general hilarity of life. And, up to a point, it can make the imbiber humorous and quick-witted. Like the Scottish football fan in Stuttgart who has had a few too many, is slightly unsteady on his feet, but is attempting nevertheless to carry a tray laden with drinks across a crowded bar.

The barmaid, fearing an accident and also slightly disapproving in a Hun-at-the-Till kind of way, says to him: 'You are staggering!' He replies: 'Thanks, hen. Yir no bad looking yirsel.'

You are never too young to start with the repartee in a pub. A precocious nine-year-old goes into a bar and shouts to the waitress to bring him a pint of lager. The woman looks at the height of him and asks: 'Do you want to get me into trouble?'

'Maybe later,' he says, 'but get me that pint first.'

Excess of drink can lead to irrational behaviour. Like the Skye man who would sit up late into the night in his croft demolishing a bottle of Talisker. His sessions often involved him phoning the manse and he would say: 'Minister, I'm very concerned about the terrible schisms in the church.'

Tiring of these phone calls but attendant to his flock, the minister told the parishioner to come to the manse the next day to discuss the matter.

The next time the man phoned drunk, the minister asked why he had not come to see him. 'It's a funny thing, minister,' he replied, 'but when I'm sober in the morning I'm not at all worried about the terrible schisms in the church.'

During the office party season, I quite often go sober and come over all morose. It's called FSAD: festive seasonal affective disorder.

My idea of Christmas cheer is hearing the tales of erratic conduct occasioned by excess festivity. One lady woke up the next morning to the horrible thought that she had been sick in her handbag. After closer examination, she was relieved to discover it was not puke but her dessert from the dinner the night before. Apparently, in her state of repletion and befuddlement, she thought it was a good idea to pop her plate of tiramisu into the Prada.

Alcohol can negatively affect the ability to control bodily functions. A chap was explaining to his wife that the vomit on his dinner jacket was not his fault. A fellow diner had been been violently sick all over him.

And, the chap said elaborating his tale, the guilty party had given him £20 to have the jacket cleaned.

'Well,' said the wife picking up the trousers from the floor, 'you'll need to get another £20 from him. He's crapped in your pants as well.'

Many of these stories may be apocryphal, but from real life I recall a colleague very much the worse for wear who had finally been detached from the festivities and dispatched home in a taxi. But her journey ended after only a couple of hundred yards when she was ejected from the vehicle. This can happen when a taxi driver asks your address and you reply: 'What the f*** has it got to do with you?'

It is usually a good idea to remember where you live. A young woman took a taxi from the city many miles into the suburbs. On arrival she proceeded to apologise to her father about getting in so late and in such a terrible state of inebriation. Her father told her not to worry and that these things happen. He was slightly more concerned that she had apparently forgotten she had got married three months before and now lived in a flat in the city centre with her husband who, by now, was probably getting quite worried as to her whereabouts.

A wife wakened by crashing noises went downstairs to find her dear husband staggering around, with his bank card in his hand. Oblivious to his surroundings, he explained that he was trying to find the cash machine.

Another chap, overly refreshed from the office party, had managed to make the taxi journey home but failed to negotiate the final part of the journey from front gate to front door. Alerted by the sound of snoring, his wife found him asleep on the lawn. She doused him with a basinful of water, as you would. He gradually came to and made his way to the matrimonial bedroom where he explained to his wife that he couldn't get a taxi and had been caught in a shower of rain as he walked home.

It's a terrible thing, drink. I discovered at an early age it could also be profitable.

Househillwood, where I was brought up, was one part of a huge housing scheme on the south-western approaches of Glasgow. About 60,000 people lived there, the population of a sizeable town in its own right. But the city fathers who had built this and other such housing estates on the outskirts failed to provide any social infrastructure. In a place the size of Perth, there was not a single pub. So the natives on the reservations had to travel to partake of some firewater.

In those days, Glasgow's pubs closed at 9 p.m., so there was a mad bout of panic drinking as customers tried to get as much bevvy down their throats before chucking out time. Then they had to get home. Which meant there were hundreds of very drunk people, almost exclusively men, falling off buses at the Peat Road roundabout, the transport hub of Househillwood.

The police courts in Glasgow of a Saturday morning used to be full of people charged with being drunk and incapable. The urchins of Househillwood were proactive in preventing such court appearances.

Drunk man staggers off bus and is incapable of walking home. Urchins help the afflicted person to his feet and guide him to his gate or close. Urchins receive thruppence or a even a tanner for their Samaritan intervention. It's a good deal all round.

Another, but less frequent, business opportunity for Houshillwood Urchins plc involved the heavy fog or smog which occasionally used to envelop industrial Glasgow in the 1950s. Again the Peat Road roundabout was the focus of activity.

There were six exits off this big roundabout. Drivers who could not see a yard in front of them were all but stranded.

Enter a couple of wee boys who approach the motorist and offer to guide the car to the required turn off. Grateful drivers give large gratuity. We returned home with our pockets full but our faces encrusted in soot from the smog and looking, as my sister said, like 'something out of the Black and White minstrels'.

We don't get smog now and we don't have TV programmes where white men black up to sing like Al Jolson.

There is nothing remotely funny about drink when a man blows half his wages in the pub on pay-day. We were lucky. My father didn't frequent pubs. All the money from his pay packet went into the family.

Others were not so lucky. Some men seemed to have an automatic self-destruct button which was activated when they got their wages. They seemed to take a perverse pride in their ability to spend almost all of their cash on a Friday night. Sipping on a hair of the dog on a Saturday morning, they would say: 'What a state I was in last night.' They seemed unfazed by the fact that they had spent not only all their own pocket money but a large chunk of the family budget for little luxuries such as food, gas, electricity and clothes for the children.

A legendary lady ran the Bull pub in Paisley. She had a firm rule that any man who had come in straight from the pub on pay-day was allowed only two pints of beer. Then they were told to go home and give the wife her housekeeping money. Many did. Some just went to the next pub and carried on drinking.

There was one extreme case where the wife and children, fed up with dad pouring all the money down his throat, on pay-day would cover every exit from the factory where he worked. The recidivist drinker would avoid the family by climbing over the factory wall to take his wages to the pub.

Legend has it that on pay-day, a van could be found parked outside a Glasgow shipyard. Inside was a comptometer machine exactly similar to the one in the shipyard pay office. For a small fee, a fat pay poke could be doctored. Overtime earnings could be removed. Even the basic pay reduced. A slimmed down envelope of money could then be taken home. Thus could a man defraud his wife and family.

Fear may have been a factor in some of these cases of counterfeiting. Certain Glasgow spouses were so fierce it would be a brave man who took home a 'broken' (i.e. opened) pay packet.

In modern domestic finance, procedures are much more transparent. The wife has her own wages. And much of the purchasing is done on credit cards anyway.

Meanwhile, back to tales of drunkenness and incapability. It can happen to anyone who, as Rabbie Burns says, goes in pursuit of sangs and clatter.

Two men out for a Friday night. One goes home relatively early, the other stays out for more drink and ends up spending the night in the police cells. In the morning he appears in court and pleads guilty to being drunk and incapable.

'Have you anything to say for yourself?' the magistrate asks. 'Yes,' says the man in the dock, 'I wish I had gone home at the same time as you did.'

Student days are fertile times for ill-considered, often unconscious, behaviour. A fellow alumnus of Strathclyde University told me how he woke up one morning in bed with a dog. Not a dog as in the horribly pejorative way some men have of describing a less than gorgeous female. A dog as in a wee Jack Russell he had obviously encountered on his way home from the students' union bar.

Another student woke up with a wreath from the cenotaph in George Square. He had somehow managed to get it back to his flat without being intercepted by the police and facing a rather embarrassing court appearance.

My own first experience of being incapable through drink should have been a warning. For some reason I had become a late recruit, at the age of seventeen, to the Boy Scouts. I went straight in as a Queen's Scout. I can't really remember much about this but the motivation for signing up was that the Scout hall could be used on a Friday night for a get-together with a few cans of beer.

There were parties as well. At one of which I became very unwell. I remember having a few cans of Guinness and then it all went blurry. I suspect that my drinks had been interfered with. There was vodka on the go but I didn't try any. It could be that one of my fellow dib-dibbers was going for his Mickey Finn badge.

I woke up, safe in my bed, the next morning. But there were no knees in my trousers and not a lot of skin on my knees. I had apparently crawled home. My mother found me slumped at the doorway. I had stuck my pen-knife blade into the lock in an effort to open the door.

I should have heeded this clarion call about the evils of strong drink. Instead I took it as a lesson about the dangers of the Boy Scout movement.

17

Trust me, I'm not a doctor

Not-really-a-Doctor Tom Shields analyses some of the most popular and some of the more outré diets.

Firstly, I must emphasise: Yes, I am a doctor. Critics may carp that it is only an honorary doctorate which I received from Strathclyde University in Glasgow. I was made a D.Univ., Doctor of the University, for services to the city of Glasgow by writing a column in the *Herald* newspaper. The citation explaining my elevation to doctorhood said that the column contained quite a lot of good jokes.

I was honoured but mystified as to why my *alma mater* chose me. I assumed it was because they were short of nominees or maybe Andrew Hamnett, the then principal, had a good sense of humour.

I discovered later I had been put up for the doctorate by my friend Alan Mawn who was in charge of the university's bars and restaurants. I would argue that becoming a doctor on the strength of my involvement with the consumption of food and drink more than qualifies me to comment on dietary regimes.

The Big Z Diet

Possibly the most agreeable way of keeping trim is the Sleep Diet. You lose weight, or at least do not put on any problem pounds, by the simple tactic of staying in bed.

It's official. Surveys by various medical organizations show that levels of obesity can be cut, and exposure to diabetes and high blood pressure reduced, by sleeping longer.

A US Government's National Health and Nutrition Examination Survey of 18,000 patients revealed a definite link between waist girth and catching ZZZs. People who slept for fewer than four hours a night were seventy-three per cent more likely to be obese than those who got the recommended seven to nine hours.

A five-year study by Northwestern University, Illinois of 1,400 children from three to twelve, concluded that those who slept more weighed less and were less likely to go on to be overweight five years later. As little as one hour extra made a big difference.

The science of this Z diet:

It's all to do with hormones called leptin and ghrelin. Your adipocytes, or fat cells, release leptin to let the body know it has enough fat in the bloodstream. By contrast, an empty stomach produces ghrelin which sends the body the message: give me grub.

Lack of sleep lowers the leptin level and increases the ghrelin count. Your appetite is under a two-pronged attack by leptin saying more fat please and ghrelin announcing that the stomach is empty.

Chronobiologists (scientists who study the effects of time and rhythmical phenomena on life processes) reckon that people are fatter these days because mankind's Stone Age bodies have not adapted to our modern lifestyle.

The theory is we have reduced sleep time by nearly two hours a night compared to the real-life Flintstones. We work longer, spend more time studying, looking after children, watching television and logged on to our computers.

In the days before all of this, and before there were supermarkets and convenience food, Stone Age man (and woman) would stay awake and eat when food was plentiful. When food was scarce, they would just go for a sleep.

The Z Diet is easy to follow. Make sure you have eight hours sleep, or more if you feel it necessary.

How does it work? You go to your bed early or you stay in your bed later.

If you haven't managed to fit in the requisite number of hours in the Land of Nod, do not get up. Phone your work and say: 'I'll be in late today. My chronobiologist insists I have a lie-in for the good of my health.'

Will the Sleep Diet work? Dr Tom says: 'More than likely. After all, if you are tucked up in bed, you're not raiding the fridge for midnight snacks.'

> SWEATING PREPARATIONS.—Sweating Drops.—Ipecacuanha, saffron, Virginia snakeroot, and camphor gum, each 2 ozs.; opium, ⅓ oz.; alcohol 2 qts. Let stand 2 weeks, shaking occasionally. DOSE.— A tea-spoon in a cup of hot pennyroyal, spearmint, or catnip tea, every half hour, until perspiration is induced; then once an hour, for a few hours.
>
> It is excellent in colds, fevers, pleurisy, inflammation of the lungs, etc. It is good to soak the feet in hot water at the same time.
>
> 2. Sweating with Burning Alcohol.—Pour alcohol into a saucer, to about half fill it; place this under a chair; strip the person to be sweated, of all clothing, and place him in the chair, putting a comforter over him, also; now light a match and throw it into the saucer of alcohol, which sets it on fire, and by the time the alcohol is burned out he will be in a profuse perspiration, if not, put in half as much more of alcohol and fire it again, which will accomplish the object then rise up and draw the comforter around you, and get into bed following up with hot teas and sweating drops, as in the first above.
>
> This last plan of sweating is also good in recent colds, pleurisy inflammation of the lungs, and all other inflammatory diseases, either in recent attacks, or of long standing complaints. See the closing remarks after the treatment of " Pleurisy," also " Ginger Wine."

The Ultimate Sex Diet

If you are following that sleep regime which requires much more time to be spent in bed, you may as well have a go at this sex diet.

It's a simple concept and you don't have to spend £15 on the book by Kerry McCloskey to grasp the basics. McCloskey, a blonde and comely former model as seen on the book cover, recommends you have sex at least five times a week.

The science of the Sex Diet:

The body needs to burn 3,500 calories to lose 1lb weight. Having sex will help you burn.

Here are some estimates of how many calories can be lost by indulging in different elements of making love:

Kissing is calculated at between 120 and 325 calories an hour.

Foreplay of an unspecified variety will expend twenty-five calories in five minutes. Unhooking a bra with two hands burns eight, with one it's eighteen. No statistics are given for bodice-ripping, single or double-handed.

Fifteen minutes of oral sex will only undo the consumption of a sip of wine and on the downside, one ejaculation can contain fifteen calories.

Getting down to the nitty-gritty, the act of intercourse uses up about 100 calories. That is, thirty-five sessions to lose 1lb. If you are a less than accomplished lover whose motto is 'I would shag her in a minute . . . but it may not take that long,' then the weight loss may not be significant.

An orgasm comes in at sixty calories. Please have as many as you like.

The good news for those whose sex life is of the DIY variety (like Woody Allen who said 'I'm a good lover. I practise a lot on my own.') a work-out can consume 150 calories, 300 if conducted vigorously. But you are hardly likely in your chit-chat across the dinner table with those nice neighbors to say: 'Yes, I have lost a lot weight. I'm on that Wanking Diet.'

I have not personally checked out the accuracy of any of the calorie calculations for the aforementioned sex acts. (Isn't it odd, by the way, how the scandal-sheet newspapers in their intrusion into private lives refer to a moment of intimacy between people as a sex act, usually a 'sordid sex act'?)

I found the carnal calorific information in the *Cherry Hill*

Courier-Post newspaper of New Jersey, home state of sex diet author Ms McCloskey. The *Cherry Hill Courier-Post* in turn had sourced the information from the clitical.com website ('helping you hit the right spot'). This the New Journalism, folks. Get used to it.

You will not get thin by shagging alone, unless you are very lucky. The Ultimate Sex Diet, inevitably, involves eating healthily and cutting out processed foods in favour of lean meat, fruit and vegetables. You can have erotic items such as peaches in chocolate, but in moderation. You can eat as much celery as you like; apparently men who eat celery give off an odour which is a turn-on for women. Better than asparagus, one hopes.

If you are having a night in with a stick of celery, it is best consumed with a spicy salsa dip which contains endorphins that help you get in the mood for love.

Ms McCloskey also recommends a lot of 'floor play'.

Will the Sex Diet work? Dr Tom says: 'Of course. Horizontal jogging must be just as good for you as the vertical kind.'

The Da Vinci Code Diet

If you are an author looking for a hook for a weight-reduction book, why not get into the Da Vinci business?

Author Stephen Lanzalotta came up with the snappily titled *The Diet Code: Revolutionary Weight Loss Secrets from Da Vinci and the Golden Ratio*. Yes, the so-called secrets of old Leonardo's code which made Dan Brown a wealthy author can also make you thin.

The science of the Da Vinci diet:

Well, it's more mathematics. Lanzalotta, who is a woodworker as well as a chef, carves his dietary niche by using the principle of the Golden Ratio, a mathematical value that was used in ancient architecture and which can be seen in nature, from seashells to leaves on plants.

The Golden Ratio is denoted by the Greek letter *phi*, which is not to be confused with the other famous Greek mathematical letter *pi*. The *Pi* Diet does not sound too convincing, unless you love pies.

Da Vinci used the Golden Ratio to calculate the proportions in paintings such as *The Last Supper*. Maybe it should be called the Last Supper Diet.

So, what does the Da Vinci diet boil down to? Your man Lanzalotta says food consumption should be 20% protein, 52% carbohydrate and 28% fat to fit this golden ratio.

Once you have done all the maths, the reality is that you have to avoid cakes and biscuits, crisps, sugary soft drinks and fatty meats. You will be eating lean meats, fish, cheese, fresh vegetables, poultry, nuts and wine.

Or, as it is known, the Mediterranean diet, which Da Vinci would have followed because he was Italian.

Will the Da Vinci Code diet work? Dr Tom says: 'Absolutely. The aerobic exercise involved in carrying around Dan Brown's thick book will help you lose weight. Carrying round the entire set of *Encyclopedia Britannica* would be even better.'

The Patch Diet

There are various products which promise you will lose weight just by putting on a plaster similar to the nicotine ones which people use to quit smoking.

It's a miracle. You carry on eating while the patches turn your fat into toned muscle.

Actually, you will not be eating normally since the point of the patches is to release appetite suppressants into your system.

The science of the patch diet:

The miracle ingredients which the patches release are mostly to be found in nature. Stuff like *Hoodia Gordonii* and *Fucus Vesiculosus*.

Your *hoodia* is a substance culled from a cactus in the Kalahari desert. The local San bushmen eat the stuff to stave off hunger during long hunting trips. *Hoodia* tricks the brain into thinking the body does not require food.

Unlike chemical psycho-stimulants, it is claimed *hoodia* has no known side effects. 'It is stimulant free, will not give you the shakes, make your heart race or raise your body temperature.' Which is nice to know, if you're going to be on the stuff for a whole month.

Your *Fucus Vesiculosus* is seaweed. The common name for *Fucus Vesiculosus* is bladderwrack, which the makers of the expensive slimming patches do not use much in their advertising. Would you go on the Bladderwrack Diet? The efficacy of bladderwrack in combating obesity by increasing the metabolic rate has been touted since Victorian times.

Dr Tom says: 'This diet works best when the patch is placed over the mouth.'

The Dog Diet

This is not a South Korean wokking the dog regimen. It's a walking the dog regimen. And don't worry, at no point does it involve making a delicious stew for human consumption out of a tin of Pedigree Chum.

The full explanation is to be found in the book *The Dog Diet: What My Dog Taught Me About Shedding Pounds, Licking Stress and Getting a New Leash on Life*, which is a title that could shed a few puns.

The author Patti Lawson relates how her life was a mess. Unlucky in love, unfulfilled with her work as a lawyer, she found comfort in snack food.

Then a mongrel dog called Sadie came into her life. Sadie stole most of her new owner's snacks. Sadie insisted on being taken out for walks at all hours.

Without even noticing, Patti had been on the dog diet and had lost eight pounds.

The science of the dog diet:

No science, just philosophy. If you think your dog shouldn't be eating certain foods, then neither should you. Out goes pizza, chocolate and ice cream as good examples. Lawson instead recommends stuff you can share with your dog; such items as bean salad, brown rice, cottage cheese, yoghurt, tuna and chicken.

I cannot recall any of my pooches slavering over any of that stuff, apart from chicken. At least there are no Bonio biscuits on the menu.

Does the Dog Diet work? Dr Tom says: 'I may be barking up the wrong tree, but it seems to me the aims of the Dog Diet could be achieved without going to the bother of getting a dog.'

18

For once I wished I was a doctor

It was not the most pleasant of tasks, but I am sure there would have been no lack of volunteers if the job had been advertised. It was a time for any citizen concerned about the state of the world to step forward and say: 'Let me through, I'm a proctologist.'

I am talking about the time in 2002 when doctors found it necessary to explore George W Bush's colon. Few people, I imagine, would have wanted to miss the opportunity to stick a hopefully large and shiny surgical implement up the presidential rear-end and wiggle it about a bit.

Or even wiggle it about a lot, saying to the patient lying there without the benefit of anaesthetic: 'I'm sorry, Mr President, this will be very painful.'

Every centimetre of progress up the presidential passage would be a small step for man but a giant leap for mankind. Every centimetre and every little twist could be dedicated to some individual who has suffered at Dubya's hands.

A vindictive sort of person might accompany each advance of the probe with comments such as: 'That's for all the Texans you executed so enthusiastically in your time as governor,' or, 'This is on behalf of the Afghans blasted to oblivion when the US armed forces decided that no wedding is complete without a clutch of 2,000lb high explosive bombs and a bit of friendly strafing.'

Citizens concerned about Mr Bush's vigilante-style disregard for civil rights might like to advance the proctological periscope a swift inch on behalf of the individuals incarcerated for having a swarthy skin and an Arab name, a crime in post-September-11

3. For External Piles.—The following is very highly spoken of: Take oyster shells wash and burn them, then finely pulverize and rub up with fresh lard; anoint with this, and take internally, sulphur, one ounce, mixed with three ounces of pulverized resin; take night and morning what will lay on a five cent piece. Take every day for the first week, then every three or four days, until well, continuing the ointment.

4. Mrs. Morehead, of Danville, Ind., cured herself of Piles by simply sitting in a hip-bath of warm water, every time the pains would come on, after stools, or any other time, remaining in the bath until the pain left her. Her husband cured himself by sitting in cold water, and using upon the parts an ointment made by stewing celendine in fresh lard. I give these various plans, so that if any one fails, a remedy may certainly be found amongst the many given.

5. G. P. Rogers, of Ironton, O., has known cases cured by using the following ointment: Powdered opium and powdered resin, one ounce each, mixed with one ounce of tallow, and anoint as required.

6. Dr. D. W. Raymond, of Conneaut, O., says: Equal weights of glycerine and tannin will cure Piles, by anointing with it, and that very speedily; also cures sore or cracked nipples in twenty-four hours, and is remarkably good for any excoriation, or sore, of the skin. I know that simple tallow introduced into the rectum is exceedingly beneficial in Piles, which satisfies me that any preparation containing oil, or any kind of grease, is good.

7. I have found in the scrap of an old newspaper, the following, and it is so easily tried, and speaks with so much certainty, and is so simple, that I give it an insertion:

"**Simple cure for Piles.**—Mix one table-spoon of sulphur with half a pint of milk, to be taken every day until favorable symptoms appear, and then occasionally, as the case may require. The above is a cheap, simple, and most infallible cure for that most painful and un-

America. The green lobby might like to give the scope an enthusiastic birl in memory of Bush's abandonment of the Kyoto Treaty.

If we had known back in 2002 what we know now about the invasion of Iraq, we might have been even more enthusiastic about carrying out the procedure.

A great fund-raising opportunity had been missed. Who would not contribute to a sponsored probe up Dubya's anal canal at £1 an inch, all proceeds to Africa to help bridge the funding gap left by Mr Bush and his fellow G8 leaders? Personally I would have pledged a considerable sum for a minute or two at the controls of the colonic camera, if only to see if there was any sign of Tony Blair up there.

19

Is red wine good for me this week?

There is so much conflicting advice on the consumption of alcohol that it would turn the health conscious to the bevvy. One study tells us that having three or more drinks a day increases the risk of breast cancer by thirty per cent, which is worrying for a chap with a set of B-cup man boobs.

Then along comes a report that three drinks a day will improve your memory. I prefer this latter theory.

When contemplating whether to have a coffee or a beer in the pub, I will recall the wise words of Maggie Kalev, a research fellow in molecular medicine and pathology at the University of Auckland, in New Zealand. Her analysis of sundry human epidemiological data leads her to conclude: 'Mild to moderate drinking may paradoxically improve cognition in people compared to abstention.'

I will be able to convince myself: 'I am not here for the beer. I am here to improve paradoxically my powers of cognition compared to those who choose to abstain.'

You will want to know the science of this.

Maggie and her colleagues studied the role of N-methyl-D-aspartic acid receptors which, as you probably know, are critical to memory. They discovered that memory is enhanced when a sub-unit of the receptor, known as NR1, is strengthened in the hippocampus. The hippocampus is a central brain region implicated in episodic memory. (Yes, I am cribbing this from a science journal.)

So, that beer is not an indulgence, it's a straightener for the hippocampus. This research was carried out on rats. Presumably, no journalists were available. One set of rodents were fed a moderate amount of ethanol. A second lot were given a dose twenty times greater. A third group were given no alcohol.

These metaphorical guinea pigs were then given various tasks. One involved remembering that the white compartment in their cage was safe while the black compartment delivered an electric shock.

The moderate imbibers did best of all, but the good news for immoderate drinkers is that the rat-arsed (so to speak) fared better than the teetotallers.

The one alcoholic drink which consistently gets the thumbs-up from researchers is red wine. You can give the tannin a moderate tanning and feel good about it.

Breasts, Hard.—Apply turnips roasted till soft, mashed and mixed with a little oil of roses. Change twice a day, keeping the breast warm with flannel.

Here is some of the evidence: A team from the division of human nutrition at Wageningen University in the Netherlands studied the lifestyle and alcohol consumption of 1,373 men whose health had been examined regularly between 1960 and 2000.

The men were surveyed to see how much alcohol they consumed, what type and over what period of time. This was cross-checked with their incidence of heart attack, stroke and other health risks. The researchers concluded that drinking up to twenty grams a day could extend men's lifespan by up to two years over those who avoided alcohol.

Readers should note carefully that this healthy amount is twenty grams of alcohol, not twenty drams of alcohol a day. Twenty grams is two medium-sized glasses of wine or one pint of beer. Twenty drams is a bottle of whisky.

The Dutch research team also found that men who drank only wine and less than half a glass a day, lived for about two and a half years longer than those who drank beer or spirits, and almost five years more than teetotallers. At half a glass of wine a day, some cynics may claim that life would only seem longer.

The researchers say:

Long-term wine consumers had about five years' longer life expectancy at age fifty compared with non-alcohol users. Of these five years, about two years can be attributed to an effect of alcohol intake. The remaining three years can be attributed to an effect of wine consumption.

For the study, seventy per cent of the wine consumed was red. The researchers add: 'This suggests that the cardioprotective effect of wine could be due to a protective effect of polyphenolic compounds in red wine, but other explanations cannot be ruled out.'

Other good scientific words and phrases to use when you are pouring yourself a glass of red include:

- Stilbenes which are thingmies providing health benefits;
- Trans-Polydatin, which is one of the major stilbenoid compounds in red wine;
- Flavanoid antioxidants, which are found in red wine;

- Reservatrol, which is the important healthy substance in wine. It is a polyphenol found in the seeds and skins of grapes. They are crushed together with the pulp to make red wine. White wine is made with just the pulp, so it does not contain very much reservatrol. (Ignore the possibility that you might get the same reservatrol hit just by eating the grapes);

- Antiapoptotic, which is something to do with activation of longevity proteins;

- Angiogenic, antihypercholesterolemic, and antidiabetic. Words which can be used in sentences such as: 'Not only is this Pays d'Oc merlot fruity, cheeky and long on the nose, it's also antihypercholesterolemic and, therefore, by definition cardioprotective.'

If you are only drinking two glasses, it makes sense to choose a good wine. The bottle will not keep, so you may as well share your £20 Ribera del Duero Pesquera Crianza with other people. It will make you healthier and more popular.

Even drinking not very good red wine is beneficial. Research shows that vinegar is good for you. The acid in vinegar switches on genes that make certain fat-burning enzymes spring into action, helping to suppress the accumulation of body fat. At least it did in laboratory mice.

It may also work on humans. The Central Research Institute in Handa, Japan, says people who were given 15ml of vinegar daily lost fat, particularly around their stomachs.

The vinegar does not have to be taken straight. It can be in your salad dressing. A glass of hot water with a few slices of lemon is also said to have the same effect.

Some of the wine you get in Scottish pubs can taste a bit like vinegar. When I used to go on the wine for health reasons I found the most acceptable method of delivery was as tinto de verano. This is your basic red diluted with diet lemonade.

But I found that a glass of diluted wine led to pints of diluted wine, which led me back to pints of lager . . . and a glass or two of brandy . . . or a rum and coke.

Maybe even a nightcap of that Sardinian liqueur which has been lurking at the back of my drinks cabinet. The liqueur that is made out of myrtle berries and gnat's urea but tastes fine, really, with plenty of ice and tonic water while you're watching the last movie on Film 4 at three in the morning.

Research shows that a session of pints of tinto de verano and lager, followed by brandy, rum and Sardinian liqueurs made from myrtle and gnat's urea is not good for your health.

20

Pig's buttocks for dinner

When I hear the phrase 'Mediterranean diet', I think of large and beautifully misshapen tomatoes the size of pumpkins; the kind of tomato that would feed a small African nation.

I think of the fruteria on Carrer Llull in Barcelona where the standard unit of measurement for fruit and veg is two kilos.

If you ask for less than two kilos (which is four and a half pounds) of apples, bananas, plums, potatoes, or anything, you get a disparaging look and are considered something of a wimp. 'Five a day' to the people in the fruteria probably means five kilos.

Which makes it quite daunting to shop there unless you have a large family or a couple of pet monkeys. You also need to take a biddy cart to get the stuff home. Prices are extremely competitive and you couldn't carry home ten euros worth of stuff from the fruteria.

In Glasgow, I once heard a bloke complain about the price of chips. He had obviously not heard the phrase 'as cheap as chips'.

The cost of a poke of *pommes frites* had breached the £1.50 mark.

'Thirty bob?' he ranted. 'I remember when you couldnae cairry thirty bobs' worth of chips.'

The Mediterranean diet isn't all lettuce and aubergines. Potatoes are well represented in the daily intake. *Patatas bravas, patatas a lo pobre* and *patatas panadera* to name but three.

Bravas are deep-fried chunky chips served with a spicy salsa and/or aioli. *Patatas a lo pobre* means 'poor man's potatoes' and are done in a deep frying pan with onion and a pepper, and maybe a lump or ten of chorizo or morcilla (black pudding), if you're not really poor.

Patatas panadera are sliced potatoes slow-cooked as in a baker's (*panadera*) oven in stock, water or maybe a dash of white wine. It is unlikely that any two cooks will agree on the ingredients or method for making *patatas bravas, pobre* or *panadera*. Or indeed any of the hundreds of other potato dishes which form part of the Mediterranean diet.

Most of the guidebooks to Barcelona will tell you the best *patatas bravas* are to be found at the Bar Tomas in the Sarria district. This is nearly true. The best *patatas bravas* are to be found at Bar Tomas (also known as El Porron) at 229 Dr Trueta street in Poblenou.

Tomas up in Sarria does very acceptable *bravas* but they are essentially nice big chips with spicy sauce. Tomas in Poblenou serves toothsome cubes of potato doused with aioli, dusted with paprika and topped with bacon or chorizo, or maybe a fried egg.

The Mediterranean diet may have its chips, but at least they are cooked in olive oil and not in animal fats.

It's the olive oil that makes the difference according to the scientists who laud the Mediterranean lifestyle. Sadly, for those who consume loads of this mono-unsaturated fat in northern climes the benefits may not be great. Research indicates that it may be:

differential exposure to solar ultraviolet radiation which accounts for the disparity in cardiovascular health between residents of Mediterranean and more northerly countries. The proposed mechanism is solar UVB-induced synthesis of Vitamin D in the oils of the skin, which has been observed to reduce the incidence of coronary heart disease, and which rapidly diminishes with increasing latitude.

It's not just the olive oil, it's the sunshine which adds to the lifespan.

Other ingredients of the healthy lifestyle are: abundant root vegetables and pulses; fresh fruit for pudding; cheese and yoghurt;

loads of fish and poultry; little red meat; moderate consumption of red wine. Most importantly, all this food is natural and unprocessed.

Another salient factor is the active lifestyle, usually involving heavy physical labour, which all these gnarled and ancient but healthy Mediterranean folk pursued.

Not having fields to till, vineyards to tend, or orchards to harvest, I get my exercise shopping for the healthy stuff. It is also an enjoyable cultural exercise. An essential part of buying your food at the market is learning the etiquette of queuing. Don't worry if you don't know the rules. An old lady will soon keep you right.

Part of the etiquette is that the old ladies don't always obey the rules. This is especially the case when standing in line at a railway ticket office. You will have waited for ages and, just as you step forward to the window, an old lady will appear in front of you as if from a trapdoor.

The same will be true in a busy restaurant when old ladies will mysteriously materialise from nowhere and grab the table you have been waiting for.

The main rule of queuing is never argue with the old ladies. They deserve preferential treatment because of age and gender and, anyway, you will never win. If push comes to shove, these tiny old ladies have very sharp elbows.

The other rule is that when you join the group of people waiting to be served, they will not be in any sort of organized queue. You must ask: *'Quin es l'ultim?'* Which means: 'Who is the last before me?' When that person has been served, it's your turn. Unless an old lady decides otherwise.

Very often the old ladies and the women serving at the market stalls will come to the aid of a hapless *guiri*. *Guiri* is the word for foreigner, usually white and usually with very little command of the local language.

I find if you put yourself entirely in the hands of the market women, they will not only tell you what's best to buy that day but also exactly how to cook it.

There is a lady at one of the stalls who can be a bit fruity. 'Have a look at these melons,' she might say more in a reference to her ample physique than to the quality of the cantaloupes on the counter.

A fellow *guiri* sent to the market to buy chicken made the day for the women at the stall when he asked for half a kilo of *polla*. He should have asked for *pollo* which is chicken. *Polla* is a colloquial term for penis. Half a kilo is a more than adequate portion, as one of the old ladies in the chicken shop told my friend.

In the market, I am particularly attracted to the fish stalls as you might expect of someone whose mother was in the trade.

It is a voyage of discovery. There are many species since there is nothing from the sea or river which the Mediterranean folk will not eat. The counters are usually overflowing. At the local market, I have often seen a crab make a belated bid for freedom, always in vain. It will end up back on the counter if not surreptitiously stuffed into a shopping bag.

I never tire of watching the fish ladies descale, gut and fillet with the skill of surgeons.

There is the usual discussion about what to do with the bits of the fish I don't really want. If I am buying half a salmon or cod or hake, I have to pay for half of the head. When the head is ritually split, for some reason I am reminded of the hanging, drawing and quartering scene from *Braveheart*.

I used to say to the fish ladies, I didn't want my half of the head, plus the skin, bones, and bits of fins that are the by-products of my getting some nice fillets, but they give you an old-fashioned look and say you really should be making your own fish stock.

So, I take all the bits home. Usually, I give them to the feral cats in my barrio. Sometimes, I decide I will make my own fish stock and put the bits in the fridge for a couple of days. And then I give them to the feral cats.

One of my favourite fish counters is in La Paradeta in Barcelona. It's actually a restaurant where you buy quantities of prawns, lobster, clams, scallops, mussels and whatever, from what looks just like a market stall. The raw stuff then goes through a hatch into the kitchen to be cooked to your specification.

La Paradeta is an IKEA kind of operation. I nearly said Ryanair but the staff are very nice. You have to set your own table, fetch the food from a hatch when summoned and make your own salad dressing.

When you have eaten, you take the dishes back, return the empty bottles and glasses to the bar, and clean your table. It is a curiously satisfying process and the perfect antidote to stuffy restaurants. It's also a whole lot cheaper.

Bread is also quoted as a healthy aspect of the Mediterranean diet. Most of it comes straight from the oven at the local baker's.

There is a nice ritual which involves the man of the house going for the bread, sometimes twice a day. This is a task which I have readily embraced.

Part of the tradition appears to be that once you have purchased your French stick, or ciabatta, or Viennese loaf it is compulsory to take the bread to the nearest bar. There you have a beer or two and a chat and nibble away at one end of the still-warm loaf.

You end up with half a loaf which is better than none. But try explaining that to the family. It's better to get some more on the way home.

You don't often hear of Scottish men popping out to get the bread. I know of one who did so in the summer of 1998. He was telling me this in Paris where he was part of the Tartan Army following Scotland.

His wife had been totally against his going to the World Cup but he had to be there. Defiance was the only solution. Well, not outright defiance. He hid his bag and passport at his pal's house and then made good his escape. 'I told her I was going out to get a loaf,' he said. 'To be fair, I have eaten quite a few baguettes on this trip.'

No matter whether you are eating Mediterranean or mince and tatties, the basic rule applies about calories in, calories out. I find I usually put on weight when I am in Spain. Or Catalunya, which is not really Spain.

I become more adipose in Iberia simply because there is too much interesting stuff to eat. I am not a glutton, I merely have an inquiring nature when it comes to food and drink.

Also, the Iberians seem to eat all day. Some of them have up to seven meals or snacks a day. These are: breakfast, elevenses, a few tapas before lunch, lunch, merienda (afternoon tea), a few tapas before dinner, dinner, and, finally, a few tapas in the way of supper. Being a social type, when I see people eating I like to join in.

When you are a drinker, breakfast can be problematic. Either it cannot be faced at all, or it is a can of sugary Irn Bru and a square sausage or two in a roll. Not the healthiest of options.

In Mediterranean mode, I have two breakfasts. The first is taken at the crack of dawn and consists of my five daily pieces of fruit with a litre or so of mineral water.

Then, some time after 9 a.m., I will make my way to a little restaurant in the old fishing quarter for my second breakfast, a small plate of morcilla and chick peas sprinkled with pine nuts. There would be a side serving of grilled artichokes dusted in paprika since no visit to this family eating house is complete without having a good gnaw at some artichoke leaves.

There has to be toast and in this case it is a large slice or two of country bread rubbed down with garlic and squishy tomato and slathered in olive oil. In defiance of my dietician's warnings, I sprinkle mine with salt.

I should have a cup of tea with all this. But small family restaurants in old fishing quarters tend not to do a nice cup of tea. Instead, I have a wee carafe of robust rosado that's so dark you would think it is a red.

Yes, it's a bit early but quite a few people in the place are having wine or a beer or a brandy. It's not when you drink alcohol that counts, it's how much.

The glass of wine is especially appropriate if I'm having my other breakfast choice, mackerel marinated in oil and lemon, garnished with wild garlic and paprika, and grilled to within an inch of its life. In the absence of an Arbroath smokie or a Finnan haddie, the mackerel does fine.

A nice big slice of omelette would be an obvious breakfast choice but I seldom go there these days. This is purely psychological since I am still coping with a tragic loss. Since Juanito retired from his tiny café kiosk in my local market, omelettes have not been the same.

Juanito's omelettes were so good, lady customers would smuggle them into the home and claim they had been made by their own fair hands.

The Spanish, or potato variety, is the king; firm and chunky with a juicy but not squidgy interior. So many Spanish omelettes are dry and tasteless.

Juanito's range also included spinach, mushrooms, courgettes and he would also do you a one-off with some particularly pungent variety from the nearby cheese stall.

The Spanish omelette in Pintxo's, a tapas restaurant in Partick in Glasgow, comes close to Juanito's perfection.

The unhealthiest breakfast I have ever had in Spain was in Cadiz, the big port city in the far south. I was drawn into a cavernous, old-fashioned café, where it seemed half the population was ensconced, consuming vast amounts of hot toast with manteca.

Manteca is basically lard, and the Cadiz version contained chunks of crispy bacon. It is a heart attack on a slice of bread and sounds disgusting, but is, so to speak, to die for. I had mine with a pot of tea.

Of all the cities in Spain, Cadiz reminds me most of my own home town. Not just because of all that lard. The people of Cadiz offer a down-to-earth, almost Glaswegian welcome.

The *menu del dia* is one of the wonders, probably the greatest wonder, in Spain. The menu is the three-course meal available at a reasonable price in almost every restaurant. It is not to be confused with the menu as in the piece of paper with details of the various courses. That's *la carta*.

We apparently have to thank the old dictator Franco for the phenomenon that is the *menu del dia*. He passed a law decreeing that every restaurant must offer a cheap three-course meal for the working man and woman.

Franco passed this law because he wanted the workers to be fit for heavy labour. He also did not want them to go home for lunch (and a siesta) but get back to factory or field and get on with the work.

The menu is egalitarian. You can see workers in dirty overalls sharing the same restaurants as the men in suits. What your average person is looking for is a menu that delivers cooking the way his mum might have made it.

The first course (*primero*) is usually substantial; a big plate of lentil or chick pea stew bristling with lumps of meat, black pudding or sausage for that extra flavour, or some vegetables such as cabbage and potatoes or green beans.

The *primero* can also be a soup that is more like a stew, or a stew that is a bit like a soup. The Catalans, who use to rule bits of old Italy, make *maccarones* or pasta dishes of the highest quality.

The healthy option of a very big salad is likely to include large lumps of tuna or goat's cheese and could pass as a meal in itself.

On Thursdays the first course is paella, just about everywhere. Again, we apparently have Franco to thank for this institution. He liked to go hunting on a Thursday and for lunch he liked to pop into a restaurant for a paella. The last thing a patron would want to do is upset the dictator by not having paella.

A more likely explanation is that in the old days, servants would get Thursday off. On the Wednesday night, the cook would prepare a paella in advance, leaving the lady of the house only to add the rice for Thursday lunch.

You certainly won't have to hunt too far for paella. A handy hint for tourists is: you will want to sample this famous Spanish dish but don't pay the extortionate prices charged by restaurants. Wait until Thursday and have it as a first course in some small family restaurant. It will be made with love, preferably by the granny. Just tell her Franco is not coming and you will have his paella.

The second dish of the *menu del dia* should not really be called the main course as it is often smaller than the first. The *segundo* is usually a piece of fish or chicken or an inexpensive cut of meat. It will come with a few chips or a handful of green salad, or even just with a roasted pepper.

Some restaurants of my acquaintance insist of serving large portions for this course (a couple of salmon fillets or enough hake to feed a family of four) and you can feel somewhat daunted.

One place, which supplied a four-course *menu del dia*, has thankfully desisted from this trencher person tradition. A four-course lunch with wine, coffee and brandy is, as Hemingway might have said, death in the afternoon.

Sometimes a doggy-bag is the only option. I'll have the paella and then the quarter of a fresh pineapple liberally doused in Cointreau. Then I'll have the slices of roast ham with the *patatas panadera para llevar* (or 'to tak awa' as they say in Dundee) for my dinner that night.

'Is that *guiri* very poor?' locals ask. 'No, he's Scottish,' the waiter says. When shops are trying to impress customers by low prices, there is usually a reference to Scotland somewhere in the advertising.

By comparison with Catalans, Scottish people are spendthrift wastrels. Catalans don't have siestas. Not just because they are hard-working. It's because they couldn't get to sleep of an afternoon for worrying that somewhere out there was a euro which was rightfully theirs but not yet in their bank account.

But we were talking about *postre* or dessert. Don't ask for pudding unless you actually want a *pudin* which is Catalan for crème caramel. There is also *flan* which is crème caramel. And *crema catalana* which is a creamy custard dish with caramelized sugar.

I would shun all these in favour of any Iberian mama's *arroz con leche*, which is creamed rice with a light dusting of cinnamon. It is ambrosia, the food of the gods. Unlike the tinned stuff you can buy in the UK which is fine and tasty but is only Ambrosia, the brand name.

The *menu del dia* should be approached in moderation. I learnt this when I was a wine correspondent and was invited to lunch in his farmhouse by Miguel Torres, head of the drinks dynasty.

I had the lobster thermidor, the magrets of duck with the fruits of the forest coulis, and quite a lot other rich fare since the Torres people like to feed journalists as if they were a goose going to market.

Miguel had a couple of grilled sardines followed by a single *botifarra* (a country sausage) and some white beans.

He explained it was simple peasant food which kept him as fit as a simple peasant. He was having the Mediterranean diet that day. I wasn't.

One day you are lunching with Don Miguel Torres, wine magnate, and the next you are eating out of a bin. That's the credit crunch for you.

Making my way one evening down the wee rambla in the Poblenou barrio of Barcelona, I came upon a group of young people busily investigating the contents of two wheelie bins outside the Dia supermarket. They had found some rich pickings.

Cartons of milk, yoghurt, sausages, beef and various other foodstuffs were being stuffed into rucksacks as the urban survivalists busied themselves with a spot of proletarian shopping.

'So, what's for dinner?' I asked. 'Do you like rabbit?' a nice young fellow replied. Having confirmed that these small creatures are no stranger to my dinner table, I was presented with a dead bunny fresh from the bin.

This particular little lapin was safely encased in a stout plastic container.

It had been consigned to the refuse because it had, that day, reached its sell-by date.

It would have been a crying shame if Peter Rabbit had died in vain. So I decided to take him home and introduce his carcass to my oven.

I was giving my young benefactor a few euros to buy himself a beer when a neighbour passed by and paused to comment that times must be tough if I was buying rabbits out of a bin. But when you are living off the land and doing your bit to ensure that valuable food resources do not go to waste, you cannot allow bourgeois prejudices to divert you from your mission.

In a matter of hours, my little friend (the rabbit, not the neighbour) was duly stuffed with a mixture of onion, celery, bread crumbs, ginger, soya sauce and chopped chestnuts.

The bunny was slathered in butter and pimenton and finished off with a basting of marmalade and HP sauce. It tasted particularly delicious because I was saving the planet.

When I was a wee boy in Househillwood, we would go midgie-raking for luckies. 'Midgie' was another word for midden; nothing to do with the infernal insects that ruin the Scottish summer. 'Luckies' was the generic term for any item vaguely worth retrieving from a bin. There were few luckies because we did not yet live in a disposable society.

I never imagined that many years later I would be in Barcelona tipping a chap to midgie-rake ingredients for dinner on my behalf. Or that I would be stuffing a rabbit with celery and chestnuts.

There are days when I come over all ecological and decide that I will not shop for food. I will survive on whatever is lurking in the fridge or hiding in the deeper recesses of the freezer.

It is no ordeal. Take a few lonely and neglected prawns, wrap in little overcoats of serrano ham, and stick them under the grill.

I had such a batch of prawns once with a bimbo. When I tell you the bimbo was toasted, rubbed down with garlic and tomato and drizzled with virgin olive oil, you will realise I am not talking about bimbo as in brainless blonde but Bimbo as in the Spanish brand of pan loaf.

The prawns and bimbo were washed down with cava, a bottle of which is usually to be found hanging about any respectable Barcelona fridge.

Another day, some stray sausages, potatoes, a boiled egg and black olives were combined with mayonnaise to make a dish which I have called summer stovies.

More challenging was what could be made from an aubergine, a red pepper and a jar of Nestlé lamb and vegetable purée for babies aged six months and up. It would have to be something stuffed. I stuffed the lot in the bin.

Ferran Adria could have done something special with that auber-gine and baby food. Ferran is a most innovative chef and his El

Bulli restaurant frequently comes out top in world ratings. He also likes to cook with fridge and store cupboard remnants.

Here's his recipe for an emergency potato omelette. Take a bag of crisps and crush the contents into wee bits. Beat three eggs and add the mashed crisps to the mixture. Leave until the crisps have absorbed the eggy stuff. Cook the mixture with a little olive oil in a frying pan until the outside is a lot crispier than the crisps inside.

It is not easy to get a table at El Bulli. After trying unsuccessfully for three years, I managed to smuggle myself in as a temporary member of a Catalan gourmet club.

Ferran is famous for mixing and matching ingredients. A bit like my old granny. But Ferran does it without the benefit of a bottle of whisky, just a vivid imagination.

Here are some of the thirty or so small dishes I had on a set tasting menu at El Bulli:

- A pizza the size of a ten pence piece. The base was made from wild raspberries, topped with ginger, fennel and various herbs.
- A beer bellini; a cocktail of crushed strawberries and lager.
- A spoon-size ravioli of mushy peas in gelatine.
- A cold soup of coconut and bitter almonds topped with a cloud of carrot.
- Crisp orange blossom wrapped in chicken skin.
- Deep-fried lemon skin flavoured with liquorice.

- Stewed dandelion stalks with chicory and shavings of tuna roe topped with a lemon foam.
- Toffee-covered white asparagus with a glass of cold cream of asparagus.
- Crispy sardine skins served with vapourized sake from an atomiser.
- Canneloni of summer truffle with marrowbone jelly and chopped olives served with rabbit brains.
- Puddings included a bread-pudding ice cream with a mango wafer and an empty loaf, a pastry in the shape of a baguette flavoured with coconut and aniseed.

A pretentious food writer described eating at El Bulli thus:

> It is spectacle, humour, debate, a culinary version of the psychologist's chair where the diner's beliefs and prejudices are exposed for examination. It is Pavlov meets pavlova, where the tastebuds and the brain cells are tested to the full.

Okay, I admit it. I wrote that.

On my journey up the Costa Brava to El Bulli, the best food I had was lunch at a hotel in a small village. I had pig's cheek as a starter and cow's cheek to follow. Sadly, there were no cod cheeks available or I would have them as a fish course.

Galtes, as cheeks are called in Catalan, are the bee's knees in my opinion, although I should say I have never eaten a bee's knee. The most common cheek to be found on a plate is that of the pig.

The meat manages to be lean, probably because of all the exercise involved in being a pig's cheek muscle, but with a hint of offal glutinosity. The meat is slow cooked in the oven and flakes off the bone.

I get a good deal of exercise cycling around Barcelona looking for restaurants which have *galtes* on the *menu del dia*.

The Mediterranean diet continually poses challenges to the uneducated palate as obscure bits of animal turn up on the plate.

Tomas of El Porron in Poblenou ordered me to try the *mollejas*. When asked what *mollejas* are, he said it was lamb and pointed vaguely in the direction of his neck.

The *mollejas* were lovely, just on the edible side of squishy, in a tangy stew with spring onions. Some of the pleasure was taken from the moment when Tomas returned to tell me the English word he had been searching for earlier.

"Glands," he said. Further research revealed *mollejas* are the thymus glands, or sweetbreads as they are known in good,

When there is great constipation, an emolient injection is indicated. Take ¼ pt. of water, ½ a dessert-spoon of salt, and 1 oz. of castor oil. Retain it as long as possible. The following injection is recommended by Dr. Simmons:

Witch hazel leaves, ½ oz.; cranesbill, ½ oz.; meadow fern burrs, 1 oz.; slippery elm, 2 drs.; mix the powders well together, and pour upon them 1½ pts. of boiling water. Infuse for 4 hours, and strain it. In the morning use ½ pt. for an injection, and at night not quite so much, and retain it, if possible, all night. Repeat as often as necessary.

The marshmallow ointment is also very useful. For blind piles the tincture of lobelia is very good; so also is brandy, a little diluted, applied frequently.

It is a good plan to cleanse the anus night and morning with soft soap and water; then using tallow or the pilewort ointment, or any of the ointments for the piles. It is good to wash the anus after every evacuation. Generally speaking, the application of cold water is more effectual than warm water for fomenting, etc.; but this must be decided by the patient, as warm water in some states of the piles is very soothing.

To effect a cure, the bowels must be kept regularly open. Take Epsom salts, ½ oz.; infusion of senna, 6 drs.; tincture of senna, 3 drs.; decoction of bark, 1 oz.; spearmint water, 1 oz.; water, 4 ozs.; best manna, 3 drs. Mix, and take from 3 to 6 table-spoons every morning, or every other day. The diet should be chiefly vegetable till the disease is gone. Or, take a gentle aperient also every other night, and on the alternate night the tonic pill (which see).

When the constitution has become habituated to the disease, stimulants, as pepper and ginger, taken with the aliment, often afford considerable relief. Elecampene root, 2 ozs.; sweet fennel-seed powder, 3 ozs.; black pepper powder, 1 oz.; milk of sulphur, 1 oz.; purified honey, 2 ozs.; brown sugar, and molasses, of each 1¼ ozs. Mix the first four ingredients; melt the honey, sugar, and molasses, and then mix all together. About the size of a nutmeg to be taken two or three times a day.

The decoction of oak bark is said to be a good remedy for piles.

"Aloes," says Dr Buchan, "which form a principal part of the advertised pills, are frequently the cause of piles. Therefore persons subject to them should avoid all aloetic purges. An habitual costiveness is much more effectually and safely removed by a spoonful of castor oil taken occasionally in an evening." A weak solution of sugar of lead with a little laudanum is useful when the piles are very painful. Powdered galls and hog's lard form a good ointment. Henbane leaves powdered and mixed with slippery elm and sweet oil, and six drops of laudanum, form a good application. The pain is often removed by an emetic, or by taking twice a day 20 or 30 drops of balsam of copaiba on loaf sugar, or in a little peppermint water. The vapor of boiling water over leeks is useful.

Piles, Bleeding.—Lightly boil the juice of nettles with a little sugar; take 2 ozs. It seldom needs repeating.—*Wesley.*

Piles, To Cure.—Apply warm molasses. Or, a tobacco-leaf steeped in water 24 hours. Or, a poultice of boiled brook-lime; it seldom fails. Or, a bruised onion, skinned, or roasted in ashes; it perfectly cures the dry piles. Or, fumigate with vinegar, wherein red

old-fashioned British cooking. I had always avoided sweetbreads, mostly because they sounded suspiciously like sheep's testicles. Also, they didn't come in a tangy spring onion stew and didn't have a nice name like *mollejas.*

There is *rabo de toro*, of course, or oxtail. The Spanish kept on eating this extension of the beast's spinal cord all through the mad cow years.

In Britain it was banned but the government kindly allowed us to carry on buying the processed foods with all those additives. Such as the carcinogenic Sudan 1 colouring agent which could be found both in supermarket shepherd's pie and shoe polish.

The *rabo* does not make you rabid. I was directed to the restaurant which does the best *rabo de toro* in Barcelona by a Kirkcaldy man who has lived in the city for many decades. He left Fife for a new life after a disappointing love affair. He is fine now that he is in a *ménage à trois* with Raith Rovers and FC Barcelona.

The oxtail was delicious; fragrant even, with ingredients such as cinnamon and cloves. Your average *rabo* normally has a thick, sweetish gravy but this one came more in a broth, possibly because the chef was sparing with his addition of carrot and onion to the mix but liberal with the red wine. Eating *rabo* is labour-intensive. Once you've extracted all the meat from the nooks and crannies of the tailbone, there is much mopping up of broth to be done with crusty bread.

You will be asking the name of the restaurant and as usual I cannot remember. If you find the Fastnet Irish pub on the harbour front in Barceloneta, there is a small square behind. The restaurant is on the left-hand side.

I should warn you that, on two of my three visits, the succulence of the oxtail has been matched by the truculence of the waiting staff. The people in the bar/restaurant on the other side of the square are much nicer.

The Spanish appear to be fond of pig's ears. I tell friends and family who visit that they really should have a go at the ears, or *orejas*.

I don't tell them that I only tried them once myself. *Orejas* taste exactly as you might expect. Apart from a light dusting of pimenton and a hint of garlic, there is no flavour.

The consistency? It's just like chewing an ear; a hairy pig's ear which thankfully the pork butcher had shaved before putting into the food chain.

You cannot make a silk purse out of a sow's ear. Neither can you make an edible dish.

The *cresta de gallo*, the red spiky thing on the top of a rooster's head, is a delicacy in Catalunya. Of course, I had to try one. You will want to know what a *cresta de gallo*, or cockscomb, tastes like. Pretty boring really, but much better than a pig's ear. I think its popularity is less to do with taste than the belief that eating the cockerel's headwear is beneficial in the male potency department.

In one attempt to enliven meals shared with my more squeamish visiting friends, I had *cap i pota*. First I translated the waiter's description of the dish which was roughly 'fat and congealed pig's blood with a small piece of meat attached'. I then actually ate the *cap* i *pota* which is fine in very small portions.

I have also had half a sheep's head, or 'sheep's heid' as it is properly called in Scotland, where it used to be a popular dish.

I had the starter of half a sheep's heid at the Pollo Rico roast chicken restaurant in Barcelona mainly to wind up my fellow diner who was decidedly unwell after too many brandies the night before.

The sheep's heid had been split in two and popped under a grill. It came to the table like one of those old-fashioned TV dinners with different items in each compartment. I dipped some bread into the brain but didn't eat it.

I ate the cheek which is a delicacy and a slice of the tongue, but gave up when the teeth became exposed and the sheep gave me a gruesome post-mortem smile. On the plus side, the scenario did provide the opportunity for that old joke about keeping the sheep's eye to see me through the week.

Many Iberian culinary experiences involve eating babies. It could be a *chanclete* which is a small piscine fellow that was hovered up from the sea without getting the chance to grow into a proper fish supper.

Or it could be a baby lamb. At the Asador de Aranda restaurant in Barcelona, they have elevated the consumption of baby lamb to an art form.

My only quibble with the Aranda folk is that they go into too much detail in the glossy brochure they give to diners. I didn't need to know that the wee fellows were taken from their mother's teat and introduced to the oven at only twenty days old. I might have guessed as much from the tiny dimensions of the lamb chops.

In a recent crisis in the British hill-farming community caused by foot-and-mouth export restrictions, 20,000 little lambs were surplus to requirement. The government had a £6m plan to take the wee sheep into protective custody.

Some of their body parts would be turned into biofuels. Most of the carcasses would simply be burned.

I suggested that the lambs should be sent to individual domestic ovens rather than the large-scale industrial variety. I even suggested a recipe based on how they cook the lambs at the Asador de Aranda. It is: Take one little lamb who has gone astray. Kill it. Remove its wee fur coat. Clean out all the intestinal bits. Dust lightly with salt, add some water to the roasting tin and pop into an oven, preferably wood-fired. Eat every little bit.

The Spanish are inordinately fond of *cochinillo*, or baby pig. (They would not turn their noses up at a baby goat either. I kid you not.)

When we eat a newly-born lump of pork, we call it suckling pig which makes it sound even more delicious. As if it's us who are doing the suckling and not the recently deceased infant.

The best *cochinillo* I have had was in Salamanca at the Restaurant Felix quite near the Plaza Mayor, which may not be there anymore so don't spend too much time looking for it. The Plaza Mayor is definitely still there and worth a visit.

The wee pig did not die in vain, as we callous carnivores say. The thin crackling, the baby fat, the tender meat . . .

I admit I felt guilty. Even more so the next morning when I visited the market and saw dozens of little carcasses hanging from hooks. They look so innocent, pink and fresh before they go in the oven.

My attention was soon diverted, however, by the contents of another market stall. The produce on sale consisted exclusively of posteriors. Backsides of pigs. Buttocks. Derrière. Call it what you will but at the end of the day, it is an arse.

They were well-scrubbed arses, with the orifice cleaned out thoroughly, or the stall-holder would not be so blasé about lifting them by the insertion of a digit.

As I write this, I think maybe I am imaging it. Or it is a scene from a film by Pedro Almodovar. But I checked with the other eyewitness. There really was such a stall.

There was no shortage of customers. The Salamanca women were inspecting carefully before agreeing to purchase a piece of arse. That's not the same as a piece of ass, which was on sale at the horse meat counter nearby.

I didn't try this dish. I can't imagine how it's cooked. Possibly the same as tripe.

I don't think I would be too happy as a man from Salamanca, home from factory or field, to find the wife had made a pig's arse for my dinner.

One of the dangers of the Mediterranean diet is free food. In many places, you get a wee snack gratis when you buy a drink in a bar. In some places you get quite a big snack.

Establishments in Salamanca and Alcala de Henares are especially culpable when it comes to force-feeding customers. My favourite free tapas location is Granada.

We popped into Manolo's bar in downtown Granada for an *aperitivo* on the way to have dinner. The first glass of red wine came with a piece of bread adorned with two small slices of bacon and a fried quail's egg.

There followed such delicacies as baked potato with aioli, mushrooms fried in lemonade batter, kidneys in sherry and a wee dish of fish.

Well before the fourteenth and final glass of wine, Manolo and his wife Carmen in the kitchen had gone through the card of their normal free delicacies and were serving us portions of expensive jamon. Manolo was also pouring, gratis, glasses of rioja from his own personal stock. We never did get to dinner.

Readers may not be surprised to hear that I tend to put on weight when I am on the Mediterranean diet.

And that is without joining the old ladies for the *merienda*, or afternoon tea. *Merienda*, which is had shortly after lunch, involves the consumption of cups of thick, sweet chocolate with cakes and *churros*.

Churros are long extrusions of doughnut mixture deep-fried in oil and sprinkled with far too much sugar. *Churro* is not Spanish for 'death on a plate'. But, it should be.

Ask a Spanish lady how she likes her *churro* and she will tell you hot, long and thick and dipped in chocolate.

21

The old man of La Marcha

When I go on the Mediterranean drink diet I have to watch my elephants. If I am having a brandy after lunch or a gin and *Fanta limon* before dinner, I try to gauge how many units the bar person is pouring into my glass.

My use of the elephant as a measurement comes from the Bill Forsyth film *Gregory's Girl*. Two of the characters in this tale of lust and love in Cumbernauld are teenage sex fiends whose hobbies include going up to the nurse's home of an evening to take some snatch photographs (if they are lucky).

They are concerned with exposures, mainly of the nurses changing in and out of their uniforms, but also the exposure of the film in their cameras. One is also a camera fiend and explains that to count the seconds properly, you have to say 'One elephant, two elephants, three elephants . . .'

The dispensing of drink in Spain appeared to me to be a random affair so I got into the habit of counting how long each drink took to pour. Barmen may have wondered why this Scottish person stared so intently during the pouring process, seemed to be talking to himself, and would turn to his companion at the end and ask: 'How many elephants did you make that?'

A pretty standard measurement was five elephants. One elephant is not far short of the standard British 25ml unit. So that would be nearly a quintuple.

The most elephants I ever got was fifteen in a glass of brandy in a student bar in Alcala de Henares. I think the young bar lady decided she might as well finish off the bottle even though it was nearly half full when she started.

That was in the old days when I used to rejoice at the plethora of pachyderms in my glass. Now I fret about what those elephants are doing to my liver.

The Spanish seem to have a comfortable relationship with strong drink unlike in Scotland where the government has officially branded alcohol abuse as a national crisis. Anti-alcohol campaigners blame low prices in supermarket off-licences and long opening pub hours for Scotland's problem.

In Spain, the drink is even cheaper and the opening hours longer, but it remains a relatively sober country. You will see a lady out for shopping having a small beer with her elevenses at the market café. You will also see young people spend all night in a bar and only have one or two drinks.

I have a theory that Scots stay up drinking out of politeness. If the bar owner is kind enough to remain open late, it is only polite to keep him or her company.

In my capacity as a guide to Scottish visitors to Barcelona I am frequently asked to lead the way from a bar which is shutting to another which is still open. One party of nurses was particularly diligent in pursuit of *la penultima*. In Spain they say there is never *la ultima*. This seems particularly true of Scottish nurses on a night out.

I thought I had done well leading them to half a dozen bars, the last of which was calling a halt at 5 a.m. My last task was to put them on the underground back to their hotel. Just as we entered the metro, there was the dread sound of the shutters going up as the small café bar in the station opened up to cater for the early commuters.

If the barman was kind enough to get up at such an ungodly hour to start work, it would be churlish not to stop for a drink.

We had become used to continental drinking hours when Glasgow was European City of Culture way back in 1990. The pubs stayed open until 3 a.m. so we could have a drink after the opera. What we got was people staying in the boozer all night and falling asleep over their dominoes.

There was art involved. Some of the scenes in the less cultured

Paralytic Liniment.—Sulphuric ether, 6 ozs.; alcohol, 2 ozs.; laudanum, 1 oz.; oil of lavender, 1 oz.; mix and cork tightly. In a recent case of paralysis let the whole extent of the numb surface be thoroughly bathed and rubbed with this preparation, for several minutes, using the hand, at least 3 times daily, at the same time take internally, 20 drops of the same, in a little sweetened water, to prevent translation upon some internal organ.

It may be used in old cases, and, in many of them, will undoubtedly do much good; but I do not not like to promise what there is no reasonable chance to perform. It is well in very recent cases to keep the parts covered with flannels, with a large amount of friction by the hand; also, electricity scientifically applied, that is by a Physician or some one who has studied the nature and operations of the electrical machine.

This liniment should be applied so freely, that about an ounce a day will be consumed, on an arm or leg, and if a whole side is palsied proportionally more. In cases of pains in the stomach or side a tea spoon will be taken with unusual success ; or for pain in the head apply to the surface, always bearing in mind that some should be taken internally whenever an external application is made. In sprains and bruises where the surface is not broken it will be found very efficacious. It may be successfully rubbed over the seat of any internal disease accompanied with pain.

establishments resembled Hogarth's illustrations of Georgian gin dens.

A feature of Glasgow's nightlife these days is that you are not allowed out late if you are even slightly grey in the hair department. All clubs and nightspots have bouncers at the door who, upon detecting a wisp of Stewart Grainger distinguished grey, will say: 'Sorry, regulars only tonight,' or 'I think you've already had enough drink, granddad.'

Apparently, the proprietors of such premises don't want oldies in the place. It might deter the younger element from frequenting the place and buying alcopops at a fiver a throw.

Age discrimination does not seem to be a problem in Spain. On a late-night/early morning stroll down the Parallel in Barcelona I passed a club from which was emanating some raucous Latin

American music. The man at the door was amused when I asked if I was too old for the venue.

He said there was some energetic dancing going on, but his advice was to get in there. 'You'll feel much younger when you come out,' he said.

I have felt welcome and had fun in late night places all over Spain. There is no problem being the old man of La Marcha.

But I am happier in a bodega than in a nightclub. It must have been those intensive oenological studies in the advanced beverage management class at Strathclyde University hotel school, but I felt inexorably drawn to the investigation of Spain's wines and spirits. This is best done on-site in a suitably ancient room filled with wine barrels and serried ranks of aged bottles.

I was lucky enough to have one such establishment only a fifty-metre walk from my flat in Barcelona. I would go there with my empty plastic bottle to have it filled from the cask.

There would be no shortage of advice on the relative merits of the fruity rioja or the big fat Priorat reds, or a Catalan moscatel versus a sweet Malaga.

There were drinks to be discovered. The local vermut, aromatic and of such industrial strength it makes your Martini appear positively anaemic. The *vermut de la casa* is cough medicine with an extra kick.

Quite a lot of the old fellows in the bodega of a morning (it opened at 7.30 a.m. for the benefit of workers at nearby factories) were having a *bareja*. This is a concoction of sweet wine and strong aniseed spirit. A *bareja* is a kill or cure option. Quite often it felt like the former.

Sadly, shortly after I had discovered the bodega, the building was scheduled for demolition to make way for yet more blocks of modern flats. The patron had a display of dusty bottles of wine at clearance sale prices.

I was an enthusiastic purchaser. The bodega must have had large cellars because there seemed to a never-ending supply of these special offers. Then a kindly fellow customer explained; the owner was getting wine in from a big supermarket up the road, but the dust he sprinkled on the bottles was authentic.

The crafty Catalan was playing 'spot the *guiri*'. A *guiri* is a tourist who is there to be separated from his or her money. Our man in the bodega was definitely picaresque, which is a word I have always wanted to use.

Picaresque means of or relating to a genre of usually satiric prose fiction originating in Spain, and depicting in realistic, often humorous detail the adventures of a roguish hero or adventurer living by his or her wits in a corrupt society.

I have cut out the middle man and now buy my wine direct from Lidl.

> BLA K EYE.—This is caused by a blow or bruise. If attended
> with inflammation and pain, wash the eye often with very warm
> water, in which is dissolved a little carbonate of soda;. or with equal
> parts of tincture of opium and water. If the pain be acute, foment
> with a decoction of stramonium leaves, simmered in spirits. Wash the
> eye, and bind on the leaves; often repeat. Perhaps the best applica-
> ion is a poultice of slippery elm bark. Mix with milk, and put it on
> warm.
> To remove the black color of the eye, bind on a little raw meat;
> or a poultice made of the root of Solomon's seal. Culpepper says,
> "It is available for bruises, falls, or blows, to dispel the congealed
> blood, and to take away the pains, and the black and blue marks that
> abide after the hurt." The blackness may be concealed by painting
> the part with flesh-colored paint.

There is probably a word like picaresque to describe the name of the street where I live in Barcelona. It is called Fernando Poo. When I first saw it on the estate agent's schedule I thought it was a misprint. Surely it should be Fernando Po, as in the island off Africa named after the Portuguese explorer?

But there it is, Fernando Poo on the street sign. I have seen wee boys stopping to snigger and say: 'Poo. That's English for caca.' Me, I like to sing the Abba hit 'Can you smell the poo, Fernando?'

I wouldn't change my street name for the world. It seemed appropriate; too appropriate when the drains get a bit high in high summer. I had a soap-packaging factory for a neighbour, just a few feet from my bedroom balcony across a narrow street.

There was a petition to have the place closed because it was too noisy. I didn't sign it. Would you like a *guiri* to move into your neighbourhood and try to close down your place of work?

Besides, I enjoyed seeing the bustle of the workers. And if they didn't mind my snoring, I could put up with gentle clang of soap-packing machines.

The factory is sadly gone, replaced by a shiny block of flats.

Also near my flat was a warehouse selling second-hand furniture. The very dab, I thought. I will fill my flat with authentic Iberian artifacts.

The item I really fancied was a genuine confessional box. I wondered if it had been obtained legally. Or maybe, it was the result of the ransacking of a church in the Spanish anarchist style.

The confessional would have made an interesting item, perhaps even a drinks cabinet, but the price being asked was ridiculously high. The trader was one of those chaps who bought junk but sold antiques. He wasn't just picaresque, he was taking the piss.

He had spotted the *guiri*. Even the most rickety of chairs or humblest of tables was priced at 20,000 pesetas (or £100). 'Is everything in here priced at 20,000 pesetas?' I asked him. No, he said, there's quite a lot of stuff at 40,000 pesetas.

I abandoned my *Year in Provence* style plan to buy authentic antiques and have them lovingly restored by Catalan craftsmen. I hired a native guide to take me to IKEA.

Fernando Poo is in the barrio of Poblenou, which means new town. It was a new town in the nineteenth century when it was emerging as the heartland of Spanish industry.

The big textile factories and engineering works have gone. Blocks of flats and offices have taken their place, but the spirit of Poblenou lives on. As a physical reminder, the various factory chimneys have been preserved.

From the rooftops of Poblenou, you can see in the distance the spires of the Sagrada Familia, Gaudi's cathedral which has become the emblem of Barcelona. The chimneys dotted about the landscape form a simple and elegant counterpoint to Gaudi's elaborate spires.

This chapter is supposed to be about Mediterannean food and drink, so I will end with details of a Poblenou protest.

The Barcelona *ajuntament* (that's the council) decided that Poblenou was to be the home of bcn22@. The idea was that you take the postcode, add the @, and you create a high-tech area with publishing, film, television, music and other industries attracted into an all-new, all-digital communications environment.

Despite the industrial decline, the centre of Poblenou has largely survived. Its tree-lined streets accommodate a mix of old and new houses, medium-sized factories, small workshops, shops, restaurants and schools. It has everything you need, right in your own barrio.

The *ajuntament* decided that what one of these nice tree-lined, low-rise streets, Carrer Llacuna, needed was a series of eight twenty-two-storey skyscrapers.

This is where the food and drink comes in. The citizens revolted. Banners with 'Poblenou is not Manhattan' and 'Say no to the speculators' appeared on balconies. Poblenou was an anarchist redoubt during the civil war and no stranger to direct action.

Part of the protest against the skyscrapers was a *botifarrada* which, as a part-time resident, I felt obliged to attend. It turned out to be my favourite kind of sit-down protest: a lunch.

Part of the threatened tree-lined street had been cordoned off, tables and chairs set up for the lunch and a stage for the speeches. Activists were busy preparing the lunch of tomato bread, barbecued *botifarras* (the incomparable Catalan sausage) with garlicky beans, chocolate mousse for pudding and a large glass of wine.

The word *botifarra* also means that rude gesture with the fist clenched and lower arm raised mimicking another part of the anatomy.

The people united for lunch will never be defeated. The council relented and the office blocks would be relatively low-rise constructions.

It is a hard life being torn between the two cities of Glasgow and Barcelona. It is even harder for those in Glasgow unfortunate enough to catch me in Bore-celona mode. As my doctor said the last time I returned to Glasgow with enthusiastic tales of sunshine, seafood and sangria: 'Be careful, you could end up with bruising.'

22

Lose weight, loose skin

I take a dim view of fad diets but a regime that worked for me was by Paul McKenna, the hypnotist bloke off the telly. Mr McKenna would likely take exception to the description of him as a hypnotist.

What he does is weight-loss mind-programming. His book *I Can Make You Thin* came with a CD which was supposed to reprogramme my unconscious mind. Every time I listened to it I fell asleep.

If I was reprogrammed, I was not conscious of it. The book contained many mind devices to help the reader change attitudes to food and drink. There were techniques to deal with cravings.

To cope with my cravings for pints of lager, I was to train myself to think of a pint of lager as a glass full of maggots. It didn't really work. I quite often thought: 'I could fair go a pint of that lager with the maggots in it.'

I did lose weight following Mr McKenna's advice. Not from his mind games but from his four golden rules about eating.

McKenna says in his book:

There are only four things you need to do to be thin for life.

1. Eat whenever you are hungry.
2. Eat whatever you want, not what you think you should.
3. Eat consciously and enjoy every mouthful.
4. Stop when you think you are full.

I think it's the 'stop eating when you think you are full' bit that makes Mr McKenna's regime such a success. Eating less will do it every time. I lost half a stone in a month just by stopping eating when I still felt a teeny bit hungry.

I could probably have lost more and not put any of it back on if I had been able to get my head around the book's instructions on using the power of the imagination to think yourself thin.

I don't think I was ready for Mr McKenna's message about continual positive change. It doesn't fit in with my default Scottish mode: 'Gonnae gie us a break?'

If my willpower fails, as it might, I may have to take recourse to the gastric band. This is a device which tells you in no uncertain terms when it is time to stop eating.

A laparoscopic adjustable gastric band, also known as a Lap-Band, is an inflatable silicone device that is placed as a noose around the stomach. It converts the stomach into an hour-glass shape. In its new configuration, the stomach accommodates much less food. The brain gets the message that the person is full. Eventually, the patient gets an hour-glass figure.

The band is inserted via laparoscopic, or keyhole, surgery. The surgeons do not get to carve your innards. When they eventually remove the gastric band, your stomach goes back to its previous shape.

The silicone noose is adjustable, without surgery, which allows the patient to decide how far to tighten the belt. The weight loss process is not as easy as it sounds. It requires significant motivation. Like when you are having lunch with friends and the gastric band tells you that your stomach is full after half a bowl of soup. You watch fellow diners move on to the fillet steak and sauté potatoes. Literally, you could not eat another thing.

I have observed a friend change his size and shape and his life thanks to the laparoscopic surgery. He is very attached to his gastric band.

There is another device which is a touch less subtle than the gastric band. It is the Anti-Eating Face Mask. (USA patent 4344424). This bit of kit does what it says on the tin. It is a metal cage which fits over the mouth. The premise is simple. If you don't eat, you don't get fat.

The science, such as it is: 'An anti-eating face mask which includes a cup-shaped member conforming to the shape of the mouth and chin area of the user, together with a hoop member and straps detachably engageable with a user's head for mounting the cup-shaped member in overlying relationship with the user's mouth and chin area under the nose thereby preventing the ingestion of food by the user.'

You may recognise the device. It is remarkably similar to the

United States Patent [19]

Barmby

[11] **4,344,424**

[45] **Aug. 17, 1982**

[54] **ANTI-EATING FACE MASK**

[76] Inventor: **Lucy L. Barmby,** 9550 Jackson Rd., Sacramento, Calif. 95826

[21] Appl. No.: **134,557**

[22] Filed: **Mar. 27, 1980**

[51] Int. Cl.³ **A61F 5/56**
[52] U.S. Cl. **128/136**
[58] Field of Search 128/133, 136, 137

[56] **References Cited**

U.S. PATENT DOCUMENTS

853,025	5/1907	McCalmont	128/133
1,297,842	3/1919	Harllee	128/136
1,629,892	5/1927	Storms	128/136
2,276,612	3/1942	Ellis	128/136
3,189,073	6/1965	Todd	128/133
3,818,906	6/1974	Stubbs	128/136

Primary Examiner—Kyle L. Howell
Assistant Examiner—C. W. Shedd
Attorney, Agent, or Firm—Blair, Brown & Kreten

[57] **ABSTRACT**

An anti-eating face mask which includes a cup-shaped member conforming to the shape of mouth and chin area of the user, together with a hoop member and straps detachably engageable with a user's head for mounting the cup-shaped member in overlying relationship with the user's mouth and chin area under the nose thereby preventing the ingestion of food by the user.

2 Claims, 3 Drawing Figures

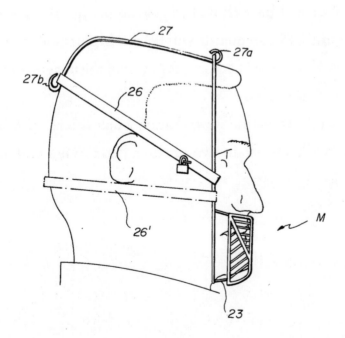

one Hannibal Lecter was made to wear because of his penchant for eating liver fresh from other people's bodies or lightly poached in red wine with some fava beans.

There is an absolutely foolproof way to lose weight and never put it back on. It's called the Calories In, Calories Out Diet. If you burn more calories than you take in, you will lose pounds. And gain pounds (sterling) by spending less on food and drink and on bizarre diet regimes.

If you eat a bit less and exercise more and have a negative imbalance of 500 calories a day, you will lose a pound in a week. To create this 500-calorie a day gap means not having a second pint of lager or a packet of crisps. It means going for an extra half-hour walk a day.

To achieve my aim of not dying too soon or at least to be a healthy corpse, I have chosen to give up my usual Far Too Much of Everything Please diet. It will be the Minus 500 daily regime. With a wee bit of Paul McKenna's power of the imagination thrown in.

I can see in my mind's eye that, if I manage to stick to it and lose about 1lb a week, in two or three years time I will be a teenager again.

23

Don't buy a round much, anymore

The Scottish government, in common with many other countries, is trying to persuade its people not to die of drink. As part of the publicity campaign to this end, we have been treated to some scary statistics. A National Health Service survey revealed that twice as many Scots as previously thought are dying through drink. There is an alcohol-related death every three hours in Scotland. Researchers had re-examined the mortality statistics gathered in the Scottish health survey of 2003 and now estimated that 2,882 deaths – one in every twenty – could be attributed to alcohol.

The team identified fifty-three causes of death in which drink played a part. It's official. There are more than fifty ways to leave your liver, traumatise other vital organs, and lose your life.

The government list of nineteen causes of death wholly attributable to excessive drinking includes alcoholic polyneuropathy, myopathy, cardiomyopathy, gastritis, liver disease, and chronic pancreatitis. There is also alcohol poisoning, plain and simple. And, for the newly-born, fetal alcohol syndrome.

On the menu of thirty-four conditions in which death is partly attributable to alcohol consumption, you can pick from nine different cancers, including: larynx, lip or liver, bile-duct, breast or bowel.

Other options are coronary heart disease, cardiac arrhythmias, and strokes, both hemorrhagic and ischaemic.

There is also Wenicke's encephalopathy, pseudo Cushing's syndrome, and Mallory-Weiss syndrome. I don't know what any of these are, except Cushing's syndrome which may have something to do with Hammer horror films. But they are all available at your local pub or off-license. Just ask for a large Wenicke with a Mallory-Weiss chaser.

A common way to go is when your cirrhosis causes fatal bleeding from oesophageal varices. Which is drowning in your own blood.

Equally common is death from choking in your own vomit during or after a drinking binge. Quite a lot of young people die this way.

You will have heard of the dyslexic non-drinker who choked in his own Vimto. I thought I would drop that one in to lighten proceedings up a bit.

There are other quick ways to end your life with the help of alcohol. Drink-driving will kill you and maybe your passengers and the odd pedestrian. For the accident-prone drinker, there is the prospect of death by drowning, fire, freezing, or falling. A journalist friend suffered the last in that list. He had left Scotland and found his own version of paradise in Hanoi where he was teaching Vietnamese journalists to write tabloid headlines. The people in Hanoi were gentle and friendly. The living was easy and he was able to enjoy a glass of beer or wine or both. He had people to look after his house. But instead of getting the Hanoi handyman to replace a light bulb, he got the ladder out and did it himself. He fell and died.

It is an object lesson on the dangers of changing light bulbs.

But despite all these grim warnings of drink-induced grisly ends, there remains scepticism on the part of many people and a refusal to face facts. We all know some old fellow who drank a bottle of whisky a day, smoked forty fags, and lived until he was ninety-three. In Winston Churchill's case it was brandy and cigars.

And it is well known that the committee of doctors tasked by the government to set a safe level of alcohol just plucked the figure of twenty-one units a week out of mid-air, with no scientific evidence.

Dr Peter Terry, chairman of the British Medical Association in Scotland and a key figure in the campaign to moderate drinking, says that the evidence is all too clear. 'The number of deaths related to alcohol is staggering,' he says with no pun intended. 'The situation is unacceptable. The consumption of even relatively small amounts of alcohol will damage your health. There is what is called category A evidence which is published in the *Journal of Epidemiology* and other medical and scientific publications. Category B evidence is what some bloke tells you in the pub.'

Dr Terry likes the occasional glass of decent wine. Sometimes he has a second glass but would rarely venture as far as a third.

The tactics of the drink-in-moderation campaigners include making alcohol more expensive, banning special offers in pubs and supermarkets, putting restraints on advertising, and generally creating a climate where drunkenness is socially unacceptable.

The problem is that these aims cannot be achieved by legislation alone. The legislation will be seen as the thin end of a prohibition wedge. Scotland's famously unhealthy relationship with alcohol will only change when individuals decide to change their habits. Which is where the government advice of drinking twenty-one or fewer units of alcohol a week comes in. This piece of advice has been around for decades.

I recall it being enthusiastically adopted by a Hebridean man of my acquaintance. These men of Celtic temperament are forever trying and failing to be more temperate. I know how they feel. It's easy to give up drink. I have done so hundreds of times. It is the staying off that is difficult.

My friend, a Skyeman, decided to follow the government advice to the letter. This meant he had to log in a diary the details of every drink he took. Things were going so well up to lunchtime on Monday, the first day of his new regime. Then a friend from back home arrived in Glasgow and requested his presence in the pub. He had a drink just to be sociable. He dutifully filled in every pint and whisky. Well before the afternoon session was over, he had consumed his weekly allowance of twenty-one units. Another attempt to go on the tack had failed. Even worse, the evidence of failure was there to see in black and white.

Me? Despite my health warnings I am still drinking in the last chance saloon.

I am trying to stick to those twenty-one units. That works out at eight pints of Tennent's lager a week. Which is a pint a day, two on Friday. I managed for quite a few months to observe the limit. But I do slip back to old ways. Alcohol is insidious that way.

If the moderation does not work, self-prohibition is the only answer. It's either that or the bleeding from oesophageal varices and the other fifty-two ways to die through drink.

I have a theory that it is not the cheapness of alcohol or the influence of advertising that makes us drink so much. I put it down to the Scottish tradition of buying rounds.

Not many other nationalities have this bizarre system of standing a drink for everyone in the vicinity. It is a particularly galling situation if, like me, you have a careful streak when it comes to spending money in the pub.

It is your turn to buy a round and suddenly there are so many recipients involved you think a coach party of friends and acquaintances and hangers-on has arrived. Then you have had enough, really, but you hang on in the pub waiting for a drink from the guy with the short arms and the long pockets who hasn't bought a round since the Pope was an altar boy.

I have given up the Scottish tradition of buying rounds. I sometimes drink too much, but I am definitely spending less.

24

Walking and bicing

The National Health Service spends a lot of time and money looking after me. They have even given me a personal trainer, Gary, at the Kelvin Hall gym in Glasgow. Gary is available for consultation twice a week under the Live Active scheme. He shows me how various bits of gymnastic kit work. But his main role is to ensure I don't overdo the exercise.

As part of the scheme I had to set targets and avoid pitfalls. My target is to be thin and devilishly handsome and, when the time comes, a healthy corpse. Things I want to avoid: being fat, losing my liver, and becoming an exercise bore.

In physical terms, my aim is have a body mass index under thirty which means I will not be obese but merely overweight. More importantly, on the waist circumference front, I want to come down from 42 inches to 36. To do so I have had to overcome my resistance to resistance training. I have begun a gentle relationship with a rowing machine, an exercise bike, and various devices with lumps of metal attached.

I have other options such as boxercise, body attack, and beginner's ballroom and Latin dancing. I'm going for the salsa but not the tea dance.

In agreement with Gary, my personal trainer, my main exercise will still be walking. An hour a day. It's all about heavy breathing. I have got to walk fast enough to be panting a bit. Enough to get arrested if I was making a phone call. They want me to go walking in the country. A wee bit hill and glen. But I will resist this and stick to the cityscape.

I already have a walking regime. I regularly walk into Glasgow city centre along Sauchiehall Street and into the Savoy shopping centre to buy salmon, finnan haddies, Arbroath smokies, cod, sea bream or whatever is on offer at Frank's Fresh Fish stall. Sometimes I get a rabbit. It's the closest experience in Glasgow to going to the market in Spain and the prices are much the same.

My other walk in Glasgow is all about being tempted by but avoiding food and strong drink. It is along Great Western Road, down Byres Road, and back along Dumbarton Road. The point is to exercise and stride past all the pubs, cafés, restaurants, and delis without ingesting a calorie. One cup of coffee is allowed. The main obstacle for the serious walker in Glasgow's West End is that Byres Road is a most sociable street and you have to stop every couple of hundred yards to engage in conversation.

The last bit of circuit takes me through along University Way through Kelvingrove Park. This stretch makes me think about food. I was once lecturing some friends from Barcelona about their misconceptions of the Scottish diet. These days, I told them, it's not about fried foods, sugar and too much whisky. It's about olive oil, pasta, fruit and veg, a glass or two of red wine. If you add in the Scottish affection for oatmeal, it might even be healthier than the Mediterranean diet. It was at this point that one of the visitors spotted a squirrel eating a discarded poke of chips. 'I see your *esquirrols* are still on the Scottish diet,' she said.

For some reason most of my favourite walks recently have involved food as a destination. If I was not forced by fate to live in Glasgow's West End and Poblenou in Barcelona, I would quite happily make my home in the Marais in Paris.

My daily constitutional would start in the Place des Vosges. It is the oldest square in Paris and reeks of history. It is usually not too full of tourists. One disappointed American said of the Place des Vosges: 'It was listed as a historical attraction but it is really just a square in between building with some fountains. Not much to see here. I was expecting maybe more little shops along the way I guess. It's not really near a lot and not much to see here.'

But if I close my eyes I can imagine Victor Hugo popping out for a stroll after a shift in his house at number 6 writing *Les Miserables*. Or Cardinal Richelieu, from number 21, wondering what the Three Musketeers are up to. Richelieu may even be on his way to visit his friend the courtesan Marion Delorme at number 11.

It's really quite a quiet place apart from all these historical ghosts.

Then it's out from the Place and into the bustle along Rue Francs-Bourgeois browsing but not buying in the many boho chic fashion shops.

I would stop and admire the Musée Carnavalet, which has the history of Paris, but not go in since I don't do museums.

I might buy some grand cru olive oil. I might go into a Jewish deli and try some falafel (chick-pea burgers if you're an American) but it would spoil the lunch that is to come.

The end point of this walk is 22 Rue du Grenier Saint-Lazare which is the Ambassade d'Auvergne restaurant. It is a cosy and intimate place and it is easy to imagine that many of the couples lunching there are having a cosy and intimate moment.

There were involuntary noises of the *When-Harry-Met-Sally* kind when I was there. But it was down to the aligot which is an Ambassade d'Auvergne speciality. It is mashed potatoes done with Laguiole cheese. It manages to be both elastic and airy, deeply flavoursome but light.

Beware: this Ambassade place will tempt you with lumps of country pate and rustic bread before you get into the menu. And the pudding can come in three or four waves.

Thankfully there is plenty of that place called Paris in which to walk off the lunch. The Louvre, Pompidou centre, Pont Neuf, Notre Dame and all that stuff is nearby.

It is no great penance to go for a stroll down the Bukit Bintang in Kuala Lumpur. This is a bustling street in the Malaysian capital which has managed to retain its local ambience in a city centre with many excesses of modern architecture and relentless development.

The weather is hot and humid, ideal for a sweaty workout. I sweated even more as I had to speed past one corner where a street entertainer had thought it a good idea to adorn the pavement with several deadly-looking snakes. Bloody typical. You make a point of keeping away from the dangers of the Malaysian jungle and some bloke brings a plague of reptiles to you.

The other danger on Bukit Bintang is that you will be massaged within an inch of your life. Those of a certain age who are martyrs to their feet will find blessed relief in one of the many massage parlours.

Best of all is steeping with the fishes. It is a simple process. You put your feet into a warm bath full of *garra rufa* tropical fish which proceed to nibble and gently gnaw away, feeding on the dead skin and other tegumental detritus on what are, for these little fellows, your plates of meat.

The attentions of the *garra rufa,* or Doctor Fish as they are also known, are simultaneously stimulating and relaxing. It can be quite challenging for those of a ticklish nature, particularly when the medic minnows get between your toes. A Scottish lady (no relation) made such a stramash of having her feet nibbled, the police turned up.

The fish come in small, medium and large. The sensations range from gentle pins and needles to a substantial suck.

Any walk along Bukit Bintang will inevitably take you into Jalan Alor, an adjacent street entirely populated by restaurants and food stalls. A stop for a large bottle of local beer is almost compulsory in the heat. The fine mist which some of the premises spray over its al fresco clientele is as much a treat to the hot brow as those fish were to the feet.

The fare is mostly Chinese hawker, or street, style. Every part of every kind of fish, fowl, and pig is available. Chillies, fresh ginger, garlic and spring onions are usually involved.

It's all very healthy south-east Asia cuisine. But inevitably you will be tempted to try far too many dishes. Not for nothing is one of Kuala Lumpur's favourite Chinese eating houses called Restoran Soon Fatt.

Probably the most surreal exercise experience I have had was in the People's Square in Shanghai. Despite being in the heart of a very industrialised city, the People's Square is a green and pleasant place.

At dawn when I was there, quite a few Shanghai folk had gathered to do *Tai Chi*. Others were doing ballroom dancing to a Chinese version of the soundtrack from *The Sound of Music*. I can't do *Tai Chi* though I could have given it my best at a waltz to the strains of 'Edelweiss'. But I wasn't sure of the etiquette of going up to a Chinese pensioner lady at dawn and requesting the pleasure of the next dance. Plus I didn't know the Mandarin for 'Ur ye dancin', hen?' I just did a wee bit of running on the spot to 'Doh a Deer, a Female Deer'.

One of my most pleasant walks of late has been beside the River Thames. Which I found surprising because, despite the pronouncement by Dr Samuel Johnson that if you are tired of London you are tired of life, I had happily given the place a major body swerve in recent decades.

I have been back to visit a friend who lives on the Embankment. Unlike many Scots down that way, he doesn't live on a bench on the Embankment. He has a big house, balconies and everything. His bit of the Embankment, just below St Paul's church, has been well concreted over but the history remains. When I walk along this bit of the Thames, I am walking in the footsteps of great writers. That fellow Johnson and Charles Dickens to some extent but mainly Samuel Pepys and William Shakespeare.

I had a colleague in the *Herald* called Roy Rogers. He was a lovely man who wrote about strikes in the days when we used to have loads of strikes. Roy had a fellow industrial correspondent called Bill Shakespeare. They were driving back together from a TUC conference once and were stopped by police for driving too fast. The policeman thought my colleague was taking the mickey when he said his name was Roy Rogers. Roy Rogers, as young readers will not know, was a famous stage and film cowboy whose equally famous horse was called Trigger.

'And you'll be Trigger,' the cop said to the passenger. 'No, I'm William Shakespeare,' was the reply.

Anyway, on my stroll along and about the Embankment, I pass places such as Pudding Lane where the Great Fire of London started. Other evocative street names in this general area include Garlick Hill, Cripplegate, and Clink Street.

People I meet on the walk include Dick Whittington, the bloke from the panto who really was a Lord Mayor of London. Then there is Roberto Calvi, the masonic Vatican banker who was found hanging underneath Blackfriars Bridge. A very competent suicide Mr Calvi managed with all those bricks secreted about his person.

Along at Temple was where George Orwell slept rough when he was writing about being down and out. Orwell, whose real name was Eric Blair, is in that long tradition of Embankment Scots.

I claim Orwell-Blair as Scottish because of his ancestry and the fact he wrote *Nineteen Eighty-four* on the island of Jura. I also meet Orwell-Blair on my walks in Barcelona when I seek out the places he mentions in his *Homage to Catalonia*.

Sadly, Mr Blair was not very conscious of his Scottishness. In his Spanish civil war memoirs, he refers to himself as an Englishman. Worse, he also refers to fellow fighters who are obviously Scottish as Englishmen. But you forgive such foibles of a great writer who makes you an eyewitness of the battle against Franco from the safety of his book.

My walk on the Embankment ends by going across the Millennium Bridge where I break my rule about avoiding museums and galleries by going into the Tate Modern. But I am careful not to look at the art. I then go into the Globe Theatre next door.

I was a writer-in-residence recently for nearly an hour at the Globe. Inspired by William Shakespeare, I made a few notes for this book. In the same period of time, the Bard himself would probably have penned a sonnet or a scene or two of *Macbeth*.

To get back to the subject of healthy exercise, Barcelona is where I used to do most of my walking. I don't walk as much there as I used to since the city council gave me a bike. Or, to be more exact, the chance to borrow one of the 10,000 municipal bikes.

The city has a system system called Bicing which is a play on words with bici (a bike) and bcn which is short for Barcelona. (Note to visitors: Barca is not the city, it is the name of its better-known football team.)

Bicing is a great concept. You pay about 30 euros a year for a card. You swipe the card and get a bike from one of hundreds of stands. You put the bike back in at the location nearest to your destination. When you want to make another journey, just grab another bike.

Inevitably, some of my Bicing journeys involve food. I will bici a good half-hour to Quimet & Quimet, the legendary tapas bar in Poble Sec, to make sure their flaky white tuna steak in a red pepper overcoat is still up to standard.

In Mediterranean diet mode, I may have a plate of artichoke, aubergine, olives, sun-dried tomatoes, chilli peppers and a veggie mince of chopped garlic, cucumber and capers. At Quimet & Quimet (so good, they named it twice) there are also pickled onions. Not your usual chip shop pickled onions; sweet little fellows, roasted and then soused in Modena vinegar.

There is a bewildering selection of wines, beer, and spirits in Q&Q. But being in cycling mode I stick to Cichy Catalan spa water.

If anything is going to save me from death through adiposity and liver failure, it will be Bicing and Vichy Catalan.

The Barcelona council has a number of strict by-laws for cyclists. You are not allowed to do wheelies or go faster than 20 kilometres an hour. I have no problem obeying these laws.

There is also a prohibition on cycling whilst listening to music on headphones. I quite often break this rule and risk a 100 Euro fine.

When cycling along a deserted beachfront early in the morning I listen to Nina Simone on the iPod. I sing along with Nina to 'I Got Life'. And celebrate that despite my ailments:

Got my hair, got my head
Got my brains, got my ears

Got my eyes, got my nose
Got my mouth, I got my smile
I got my tongue, got my chin
Got my neck, got my boobs
Got my heart, got my soul
Got my back, I got my sex
I got my arms, got my hands, got my fingers,
Got my legs, got my feet, got my toes,
Got my liver, got my blood . . .

I had not realised before that Nina was singing about cirrhosis, type 2 diabetes, haemochromatosis, phimosis, depression, obesity, incipient baldness, deafness, and about me.